The Best Schools

Thomas Armstrong

How Human Development Research Should
Inform Educational Practice

Foreword by David Elkind

Association for Supervision and Curriculum Development
Alexandria, Virginia USA

Association for Supervision and Curriculum Development
1703 N. Beauregard St. • Alexandria, VA 22311-1714 USA
Phone: 800-933-2723 or 703-578-9600 • Fax: 703-575-5400
Web site: www.ascd.org • E-mail: member@ascd.org
Author guidelines: www.ascd.org/write

Gene R. Carter, *Executive Director;* Nancy Modrak, *Director of Publishing;* Julie Houtz, *Director of Book Editing & Production;* Deborah Siegel, *Project Manager;* Catherine Guyer, *Senior Graphic Designer;* Valerie Younkin, *Typesetter;* Dina Murray Seamon, *Production Specialist/Team Lead*

All Web links in this book are correct as of the publication date below but may have become inactive or otherwise modified since that time. If you notice a deactivated or changed link, please e-mail books@ascd.org with the words "Link Update" in the subject line. In your message, please specify the Web link, the book title, and the page number on which the link appears.

ASCD Member Book, No. FY07-2 (November 2006, PC). ASCD Member Books mail to Premium (P), Comprehensive (C), and Regular (R) members on this schedule: Jan., PC; Feb., P; Apr., PCR; May, P; July, PC; Aug., P; Sept., PCR; Nov., PC; Dec., P.

PAPERBACK ISBN-13: 978-1-4166-0457-0 ASCD product #106044
PAPERBACK ISBN-10: 1-4166-0457-X

Also available as an e-book through ebrary, netLibrary, and many online booksellers (see Books in Print for the ISBNs).

Quantity discounts for the paperback edition only: 10–49 copies, 10%; 50+ copies, 15%; for 1,000 or more copies, call 800-933-2723, ext. 5634, or 703-575-5634. For desk copies: member@ascd.org.

Library of Congress Cataloging-in-Publication Data

Armstrong, Thomas.
    The best schools : how human development research should inform educational practice / Thomas Armstrong ; foreword by David Elkind.
        p. cm.
    Includes bibliographical references and index.
    ISBN-13: 978-1-4166-0457-0 (pbk. : alk. paper)
    ISBN-10: 1-4166-0457-X (pbk. : alk. paper)   1. Child development—Research. 2. Learning, Psychology of.   3. Developmental psychology. 4. School improvement programs.   I. Title.
    LB1131.A729 2006
    370.15'23—dc22   2006024184

18 17 16 15 14 13 12 11 10 09 08 07   1 2 3 4 5 6 7 8 9 10 11 12

The future of Bamfylde, now.
Whether it's to be turned into an
exam factory or remain a place fit for
human beings like you or me.
Now that does seem worth getting
steamed up about, hmm?

—To Serve Them All My Days

The Best Schools

How Human Development Research Should Inform Educational Practice

Foreword vii

Introduction. 1

1. Academic Achievement Discourse 7

2. Human Development Discourse. 34

3. Early Childhood Education Programs: Play 69

4. Elementary Schools: Learning How the World Works. 88

5. Middle Schools: Social, Emotional,
   and Metacognitive Growth 111

6. High Schools: Preparing Students to Live Independently
   in the Real World 135

Conclusion. 151

Appendix 157

References 160

Index. 176

About the Author 182

Foreword

What is the aim of education? Is the primary goal of schooling to train young people to pass tests and get good grades, or is it, as Jean Piaget once put it, "To train young people to think for themselves and not to accept the first idea that comes to them." This is the issue addressed in this powerful and important book. Armstrong argues that these two aims reflect different educational discourses that guide and direct pedagogical values, thoughts, and practices. One of these discourses, the Academic Achievement Discourse (mightily aided and abetted by the No Child Left Behind legislation), currently dominates the educational scene. The alternative, Human Development Discourse, is found in some public, charter, and private schools that adapt their curricula to the developing needs, interests, and abilities of the students. Schools that implement the Human Development Discourse are what Armstrong refers to as The Best Schools.

To make his case against Academic Achievement Discourse, Armstrong gives a brief history of this orientation and then lists 12 negative consequences of this type of pedagogy. Some of these negative consequences, like teaching to the tests, and inadequate attention to individual, cultural, and ethnic differences, are familiar critiques of the No Child Left Behind agenda. When all of these negative consequences are brought together in one place, however, the overall impact is so strong, one has to question why this dysfunctional educational discourse is so dominant. The answer is, of course, that what we do in our schools has nothing to do with what we know is effective pedagogy for children. Rather, what we do in our public schools is largely determined by social, political, economic, and cultural considerations. The best interests of children are too often left behind.

In parallel with his critique of the Academic Achievement Discourse, Armstrong presents a brief history of the Human Development Discourse and lists 10 positive consequences of this pedagogical orientation. Again, many of the arguments for a human development approach to education are familiar. These include the enabling of all students to realize their individual patterns of strengths and abilities, and allowing students to take control of their learning environment. Armstrong argues that while the quantitative test results of Academic Achievement Discourse offer educators a quick and easy way to document the results of instruction, the benefits of Human Development Discourse are long-term and best expressed in qualitative assessments that have equal or greater validity as methods for evaluating learning progress.

In the remaining sections of the book, Armstrong gives illustrations of how the Human Development Discourse can be put into practice at the preschool, elementary, middle, and high school levels. Armstrong describes what should be the central focus of pedagogy at each level. At the preschool level, education should evolve out of the child's play. That is to say, at this stage learning is largely inner-directed and the early childhood educator can build the curriculum around and through children's spontaneous interests. Elementary education, according to Armstrong, should focus on helping children understand how the world works by actively engaging them in real-life activities. Middle schools, when children are attaining second-order reasoning skills, should emphasize social, emotional, and metacognitive growth. Finally, high schools should be devoted to preparing students to live independently in the real world.

In these last chapters of the book, Armstrong gives many practical suggestions and guidance for developmentally appropriate practice at each of the four levels of education. He also gives examples of Academic Achievement practices that should be avoided. These last chapters are what make this book different from those that deal with either theory or classroom matters. Armstrong is both an academic and a practitioner and he is able to translate the theoretical assumptions of the Human Development Discourse into practical teaching strategies and practices. As such this book is a much needed guide to the Human Development Discourse and to its application across the K–12 educational spectrum.

David Elkind

Introduction

A book with the title *The Best Schools* conjures up images of a long list of schools ranked according to some clear standard of excellence. *U.S. News & World Report* (Morse, Flanigan, & Yerkie, 2005) has done this with "the best colleges"; *Newsweek* has done this with "the best high schools" (Kantrowitz et al., 2006); and numerous Internet sites have done this with elementary schools (see, for example, www.learn4good.com). This book, however, has no such pretensions. Instead, my aim is to describe the best practices in education based on what we currently know about human development. In this book, you will find examples from more than 50 schools that are engaged in such best practices. These schools, however, are not ranked in any particular order, and many other schools could have been cited as well. In the *Newsweek* survey, high schools were ranked according to the following formula: the number of Advanced Placement and International Baccalaureate tests taken by all students at a school divided by the number of graduating seniors. There are no formulas in this book. I believe that attempts to create such formulas, and "best schools" lists in the first place, are symptomatic of a disturbing trend in this country (and across the world) to use test scores and a "rigorous academic curriculum" as the primary criteria for defining what constitutes a superior learning environment. Rather than test scores and rigor, I am far more concerned in this book with how responsive schools are to the real developmental needs of their students.

Because I am using developmental criteria to define "the best schools," I need to clarify here what I mean by "developmentally appropriate" and "developmentally inappropriate" educational practices. Certainly every educator recognizes that it is developmentally inappropriate to plunk a college calculus textbook down in front of a 2-year-old child and expect her to master the material over the course of a year. But beyond this sort of clear-cut scenario, there seems to be a wide range of interpretations of what "developmentally appropriate" actually means. I have seen arguments made for the belief that scripted learning and direct instruction are developmentally appropriate practices (Kozloff & Bessellieu, 2000). I disagree.

I have also noted that some practices that were considered developmentally inappropriate a decade or two ago are now suddenly deemed developmentally appropriate. One good example involves standardized testing in early childhood education programs. In 1987, the National Association for the Education of Young Children (NAEYC) published a position paper that cautioned against most standardized testing for children under the age of 8. Sixteen years later, however, NAEYC abandoned this position and instead made a key recommendation in a position paper to "make ethical, appropriate, valid, and reliable assessment a central part of all early childhood programs" (2003, p. 10). Similarly, 16 years ago, when I was writing an article about computers and young children for a national parenting magazine (Armstrong, 1990), most child development experts that I contacted cautioned against any computer use before age 4. Now, it would seem like heresy to suggest that 3-year-olds should be deprived of the opportunity to prepare for a high-tech future. I will, however, suggest that very thing in Chapter 3 of this book.

The changes in the definition of what is considered "developmentally appropriate" over the past two decades have occurred, I believe, because of the growing dominance of what I'm going to call in this book "Academic Achievement Discourse." Words and phrases used in this discourse include "accountability," "standardized testing," "adequate yearly progress," "No Child Left Behind," "closing the achievement gap," and "rigorous curriculum." In Chapter 1, I discuss in detail the core components, history, and problems with this almost universally embraced discourse in education. In Chapter 2, I strongly urge educators to leave this narrow definition of learning behind and return instead to the great thinkers of human development that have informed educational practice over the past 100 years—Montessori, Piaget, Freud, Steiner, Erikson, Dewey, Elkind, Gardner—and to the newest findings in how the brain develops over the course of childhood and adolescence. In this way, we might fashion a renewed discourse in education: a Human Development Discourse. In this discourse, educators and educational researchers are required to pay close attention to the vast qualitative differences that exist in the physical, emotional, cognitive, and spiritual worlds of preschoolers, elementary school students, young teens, and high school students, and to develop educational practices that are sensitive to these differing developmental needs.

It almost seems as if these days the term "developmental" has come to mean "how students perform on pre-tests compared to how they perform on post-tests." As a result, the term "developmentally appropriate practices" no longer means what sorts of educational practices children at different ages *should* be engaged in, but what practices they *can* engage in. Because research shows that 3-year-olds can learn a lot from a computer, this becomes, ipso facto, "developmentally appropriate," despite the fact that their actual *needs* require rich interactions with the sensory world and not a "virtual world" at all.

In this book, I propose that educators focus on one particular developmental need at each of the four main levels of formal education: early childhood, elementary, middle school, and high school. In Chapter 3, I suggest that *play* is the crucial need for preschoolers and kindergarteners, and that current high pressure academic practices in early childhood education be abandoned as harmful to their growth and development. In Chapter 4, I suggest that the central developmental issue for children at the elementary school level is *learning how the world works* and that practices that take children at this age away from the world (and into artificially contrived learning environments) are developmentally misguided. In Chapter 5, I highlight the crucial importance of puberty and the need for educational practices that focus on *social, emotional, and metacognitive learning* to create developmentally appropriate practices at the middle school level. Finally, in Chapter 6, I suggest that "developmental high schools" (a term that ought to be used, just as we speak of "developmental kindergartens") should ultimately focus on helping students *prepare to live independently in the real world*. Please note that I am not suggesting that these are the *only* developmental issues that are important at each level.

Similarly, I want to make clear that *each* of these goals are important for *all* students regardless of their developmental level. High school students should be playful in their learning, just as preschoolers need to develop socially, emotionally, and even meta-cognitively (e.g., when they are playing "king of the mountain"). However, I do want to emphasize that there are developmental features specific to each level (e.g., the uncommitted cortex of preschoolers, the broader social context of elementary school children, the experience of puberty in early adolescence, and the proximity to adulthood of high school students) that make each goal that I have selected especially important as a focus in creating best practices in the schools.

What compels me to write this book is my grave concern that pressures on students at all levels to achieve academically are causing educators to ignore the true developmental needs of children and adolescents. The push for higher test scores and the demand that *all* students exhibit high proficiency in reading, math, and science is sending reverberations throughout all levels of education, creating stressed-out 12th graders, violent 8th graders, attention-deficit 3rd graders, and 4-year-olds who have had their childhoods stripped away from them. This situation cannot be allowed to go on as it is. It's time that we returned to the great questions of human growth and learning: How can we help each child reach his or her true potential? How can we inspire each child and adolescent to discover his or her inner passion to learn? How can we honor the unique journey of each individual through life? How can we inspire our students to develop into mature adults? If educators lose touch with these questions in their mad dash to boost test scores, then culture as we know it may truly cease to exist some day. This book is written in the hope that such a day never comes, and that we instead regard the optimal and natural development of children and adolescents as our most sacred duty as educators and our ultimate legacy to humanity.

1

Academic Achievement Discourse

These are difficult times for educators who believe that learning is worth pursuing for its own sake and that the chief purpose of school is the nurturing of students as whole human beings. Higher test scores seem to be the order of the day. To accomplish this aim, administrators strain to meet political agendas, teachers respond by teaching to the test, and students in turn react by cheating, taking "learning steroids" (legal and illegal psychostimulants), or just not caring in order to cope with the demands placed on them in school. The adventure of learning, the wonder of nature and culture, the richness of human experience, and the delight in acquiring new abilities all seem to have been abandoned or severely curtailed in the classroom in this drive to meet quotas, deadlines, benchmarks, mandates, and targets.

The immediate cause of this crisis in education is the No Child Left Behind Act of 2001 (NCLB), which greatly expanded the role of the federal government in determining what goes on in the classroom. Its many provisions include annual testing of students in reading and mathematics (and starting in 2007, testing in science as well), and the requirement that schools make adequate yearly progress (AYP) incrementally on a year-by-year basis until *all* students reach 100 percent proficiency in these areas by the year 2014. Failure of a school to maintain AYP will result in penalties for the school, including the right of students to receive special tutoring or to transfer to schools that *do* maintain AYP, and the eventual placement of a school on probation leading to possible government or commercial takeover. Although NCLB has been hailed by many groups as a major step toward narrowing the achievement gap for poor and minority populations, its actual implementation has revealed a significant cluster of difficulties (see for example, Archer, 2005; Karp, 2003; Klein, 2006; Lee, 2006; Olson, 2005).

Aside from any specific problems inherent in the law itself, however, what seems most troubling about NCLB is that it represents the culmination of a movement that has been gathering steam in American education for over 80 years. The most destructive legacy of NCLB may turn out to be that it hijacks the dialogue in education away from talking about the education of human beings (what I'm going to call in this book "Human Development Discourse") and toward a focus on tests, standards, and accountability (what I will refer to as "Academic Achievement Discourse"). In this chapter, I will define the implicit assumptions of Academic Achievement Discourse, explore its history in U.S. education, and detail the way it sabotages the efforts of educators to make a positive and lasting impact on the lives of students. In the next chapter, I will explore the assumptions, history, and positive consequences of engaging in Human Development Discourse. If we are to understand what conditions underlie the best schools in our country, we need to clarify whether we are talking about schools with the highest standardized test scores and adequate yearly progress, or whether there are other more human and *humane* elements that need to be taken into consideration.

Academic Achievement Discourse: A Definition

First let me explain what I mean by the term "discourse." The word "discourse" as a noun is defined in the *Oxford English Dictionary* as "communication of thought by speech," "the faculty of conversing," or "a spoken or written treatment of a subject" (Simpson & Weiner, 1991, p. 444). In the field of philosophy and in the social sciences, the word has a more specific designation:

> A discourse is considered to be an institutionalized way of thinking, a social boundary defining what can be said about a specific topic. . . . Discourses are seen to affect our views on all things; in other words, it is not possible to escape discourse. For example, two distinctly different discourses can be used about various guerrilla movements describing them either as "freedom fighters" or "terrorists." In other words, the chosen discourse delivers the vocabulary, expressions, and perhaps also the style needed to communicate. (Wikipedia, n.d., para. 1)

In the field of education, one might engage in a "disability discourse" (seeing a child primarily in terms of what he or she *can't* do, through labels such as "learning disability" or "attention deficit hyperactivity disorder") or a "learning differences discourse" (seeing a child primarily in terms of how he or she learns, with an effort not to label but to describe the child's specific ways of thinking and learning as accurately and specifically as possible). In other words, two educators can be looking at the same student and engage in vastly different speech acts and written communications about that student.

In my previous writings, I have devoted a great deal of time to delineating the differences between these two particular kinds of discourse (see, for example, Armstrong, 1997, 2000a). In some of these writings, I've used the term "paradigm" to mean something equivalent to "discourse" (see, for example, Armstrong, 2003a). I've come to prefer the term "discourse," however, because it more accurately specifies the actual speech acts and written communications that educators use to reveal their underlying assumptions about learning and education. The words that educators use to describe their students, the speeches made by politicians regarding education, and the laws that are written to enforce those beliefs are three examples of speech acts and written communications that have had immediate, practical, and significant impact on classroom practices. In this book, I will contrast two distinctly different educational discourses, Academic Achievement Discourse and Human Development Discourse. I will suggest that the types of speech acts and written communications, or discourses, engaged in by educators today—at least in public settings—are predominantly and increasingly Academic Achievement Discourse.

What do I mean by Academic Achievement Discourse? I use this term to designate the totality of speech acts and written communications that view the purpose of education primarily as supporting, encouraging, and facilitating a student's ability to obtain high grades and standardized test scores in school courses, especially in courses that are part of the core academic curriculum. Academic Achievement Discourse, however, means much more than this simple definition. There are several assumptions that help shape Academic Achievement Discourse:

Assumption #1: *Academic content* **and** *skills* **are the** *most* **important things to be learned.**

The first word in Academic Achievement Discourse tells us a great deal about what is valued in learning: academics. First and foremost in Academic Achievement Discourse is an emphasis on *academic* content (literature, science, and math) and *academic* skills (reading, writing, problem solving, and critical thinking). These are the areas, after all, that students are required to be proficient in by the year 2014 and that schools are expected to make adequate yearly progress on from year to year as part of the NCLB law. One could also be fairly confident in adding IT (information technology, including computer skills) to this pantheon.

Given an important but secondary status in Academic Achievement Discourse is the study of history, the social sciences, and foreign languages. Content and skill areas that are generally considered to be *outside* Academic Achievement Discourse (unless achievement in these areas can be tied statistically to academic achievement) include music, drama, art, physical education, vocational education of different types (e.g., auto mechanics, food preparation), and "life skills" (e.g., parenting skills or family studies, counseling and guidance, personal care, and health education). Thus, it is more important in the Academic Achievement Discourse to learn the vocabulary words for the sport of soccer than to be able to *play* soccer. It is more important to generate a timeline of the Civil War than to be able to dramatize significant events in that war. It is more important to know the names of the 206 bones in a human being than it is to know how to take care of those bones in one's own personal life through proper diet and exercise.

Assumption #2: Measurement of achievement occurs through *grades* and *standardized testing*.

The second word in Academic Achievement Discourse, *achievement,* tells us how educators want students to engage in academic content and skills. Educators want students to *achieve* in these areas. The *Oxford English Dictionary* defines "achievement" as "the act of achieving, completing, or attaining by exertion; completion, accomplishment, successful performance" (Simpson & Weiner, 1991, p. 12). Thus, in Academic Achievement Discourse, there needs to be a successful completion, through effort, of the acquisition of academic content and skills.

How does Academic Achievement Discourse define whether achievement has taken place? Its most highly valued method of determining whether a successful completion has taken place for each student is *quantitative* in nature. In other words, *numbers* (in the context of grading and testing) are used to indicate whether a student has been successful or unsuccessful in mastering academic content and skills. A student who receives a 4.0 grade point average (where 4 equals an *A*) is deemed to have achieved, whereas a student who has a 1.0 grade point average is deemed not to have achieved. A student who takes a standardized test in reading and scores at a 99th percentile is regarded as an achiever, while a student who scores at a 14th percentile is seen as a nonachiever.

Assumption #3: Academic Achievement Discourse favors an academic curriculum that is *rigorous*, *uniform*, and *required for all students*.

One phrase frequently heard in Academic Achievement Discourse is "raising the bar." This phrasing implies that academic requirements are being made tougher and that academic courses are being created that are more rigorous than they were previously (through the addition, for example, of Advanced Placement courses or an International Baccalaureate program). Academic Achievement Discourse promotes a situation in which students are required to take courses deemed more difficult; listen to longer lectures; study harder; have more homework than they did before; and engage in more reading, writing, and problem-solving activities (as opposed to activities viewed as softer, such as interviewing, role playing, and taking field trips).

Similarly, Academic Achievement Discourse proponents prefer that all students in a school take the same coursework and engage in that coursework in the same way—through traditional methods such as note taking, raising hands for questions, and reading the same textbooks. Academic Achievement Discourse generally does not favor engaging in individualized instruction, taking into consideration individual learning styles, or giving students significant choices in their selection of material and methods used in learning.

Assumption #4: Academic Achievement Discourse is primarily *future-oriented*.

Learning in Academic Achievement Discourse is not generally valued for its own sake—that is, because learning itself is intrinsically worthwhile and satisfying. Rather, learning takes place as a preparation for the future. Educators want students to achieve academically so that they will be ready for something that will take place later (e.g., challenges, college, or jobs). Sometimes it is the near future that is the focus. For example, a kindergarten teacher might say something like, "I'd prefer not to have my students do so many worksheets, but I have to get them *ready* for the rigors of 1st grade." A word frequently used in early childhood education, "readiness," is a key indicator that Academic Achievement Discourse is being used. At other times it is the more distant future that is evoked. When a politician says, for example, "The low test scores in our nation's schools indicate that we are not adequately preparing our students for the challenges of the 21st century," he is gesturing toward the future-oriented dimension of Academic Achievement Discourse.

Assumption #5: Academic Achievement Discourse is *comparative* in nature.

There is a distinct preference in Academic Achievement Discourse for making comparisons *between* students, schools, school districts, states, or even countries, as opposed to looking at the changes that take place over time *within* each of these groups. So, for example, an individual student's performance on a standardized test will be compared to the performance of a group of students who took the test under equivalent circumstances at another time and place (a "normative" measure). This approach is given preference in Academic Achievement Discourse to looking at that student's individual improvement over time (an "ipsative" measure). On an organizational level, test scores are used in Academic Achievement Discourse to compare the performance of individual schools or school districts in a state. Increasingly, these results are being posted in community newspapers or on Web sites, such as www.greatschools.net, so that parents can fully engage in this aspect of Academic Achievement Discourse.

The ultimate expression of this component of Academic Achievement Discourse occurs when the math, science, and reading scores of different nations of the world are compared to each other. Politicians can then engage in Academic Achievement Discourse with a statement such as one that is included in the Executive Summary of the No Child Left Behind Act: "Our high school seniors trail students in Cyprus and South Africa on international math tests" (U.S. Department of Education, 2002, p. 1).

Assumption #6: Academic Achievement Discourse bases its claims for validity on *scientifically based research*.

When promoting its cause, educators and others who engage in Academic Achievement Discourse usually state that their teaching strategies and interventions, as well as their benchmarks and assessments, are backed up by scientifically based research data. Similarly, when defending their position, the accusation is frequently made that programs favored by critics usually *lack* support from scientifically based research. This term generally refers to statistical results obtained by qualified researchers with PhD, EdD, or MD degrees that are published in peer-reviewed educational, psychological, and scientific journals. The No Child Left Behind Act contains more than 100 references to scientifically based research or some approximation of it, and provides an even more specific definition of this term by recommending randomized controlled trials as the gold standard of educational research (Olson, 2002). To quote from a U.S. Department of Education (2003) booklet:

> For example, suppose you want to test, in a randomized controlled trial, whether a new math curriculum for 3rd graders is more effective than your school's existing math curriculum for 3rd graders. You would randomly assign a large number of 3rd grade students to either an intervention group, which uses the new curriculum, or to a control group, which uses the existing curriculum. You would then measure the math achievement of both groups over time. The difference in math achievement between the two groups would represent the effect of the new curriculum compared to the existing curriculum. (p. 1)

Assumption #7: Academic Achievement Discourse generally takes place in a *top-down environment* in which individuals with greater political power impose programs, procedures, and policy on individuals with less power.

Much of the impetus for Academic Achievement Discourse comes not from educators working in the classroom but from individuals with political power—for example, the president, governors, legislators, or CEOs of large corporations. Based on their speech acts (e.g., "our children are falling behind in the international marketplace of ideas") and their written communications (e.g., laws such as NCLB), they create a climate in which educators *must* engage in Academic Achievement Discourse. Those who are most committed to this discourse in the field of education are, similarly, individuals in positions of power—for example, state education officials, superintendents, principals, and other administrators. They in turn create an environment that requires those under them (teachers) to speak the same language, especially when they are in the presence of these supervisors and administrators. Other sources of power that generate Academic Achievement Discourse are parents, school boards, and members of the mass media, who report national test results on a regular basis. At the bottom of this food chain are the students themselves, who have little power but must nevertheless engage in Academic Achievement Discourse in their own way. For example, one student might ask another, "Whad'ja get on yesterday's test?"

Assumption #8: The bottom line in Academic Achievement Discourse hinges on *grades*, *test scores*, and ultimately, *money*.

In terms of education, the bottom line in Academic Achievement Discourse is based on grades and test scores. Students may not be permitted to graduate from high school, for example, if they are unable to maintain a specific grade point average or pass a high-stakes graduation test. Similarly, schools can be penalized under the NCLB law if they fail to make adequate yearly progress in student proficiency on standardized test scores.

At a deeper level, however, it becomes apparent that the ultimate desired outcome of Academic Achievement Discourse is
something like the following scenario: to have a student earn a 4.0
(or higher) grade point average on Advanced Placement or International Baccalaureate courses in high school; achieve a perfect 2400
score on the SAT; enter a prestigious college or university such as
Harvard, Yale, Princeton, or Stanford; achieve the highest grades
there; graduate summa cum laude; achieve the highest scores on
a graduate or professional school test; attend a prestigious law
school, medical school, business school, or other postgraduate
institution; and then (and here comes the payoff) take the most
lucrative positions in society—lawyer, doctor, business executive,
research scientist, and so on.

This type of scenario represents the pinnacle of success in our
corporate-influenced culture. However, as we will see in the next
chapter, there are other aims of education that may be equal or
superior in value to the goals of Academic Achievement Discourse.

A History of Academic Achievement Discourse

Although any history of Academic Achievement Discourse is bound
to be somewhat subjective in its selection of key events, I believe
it is possible to construct a general outline of a movement toward
increasing engagement by U.S. educators in Academic Achievement Discourse (see Figure 1.1). If I were to pick a single event that
precipitated Academic Achievement Discourse in the history of U.S.
education, I would choose the recommendations of the Committee
on Secondary School Studies (also known as the Committee of Ten)
that were published in 1893. This group, created by the National
Education Association and chaired by the president of Harvard
University, Charles Eliot, was convened in an attempt to bring order
into an increasingly diverse student population and an increasingly
disparate curriculum that had unfolded during the 19th century in
America. Especially important was the question of how much the

Figure 1.1

Key Events in the History of Academic Achievement Discourse

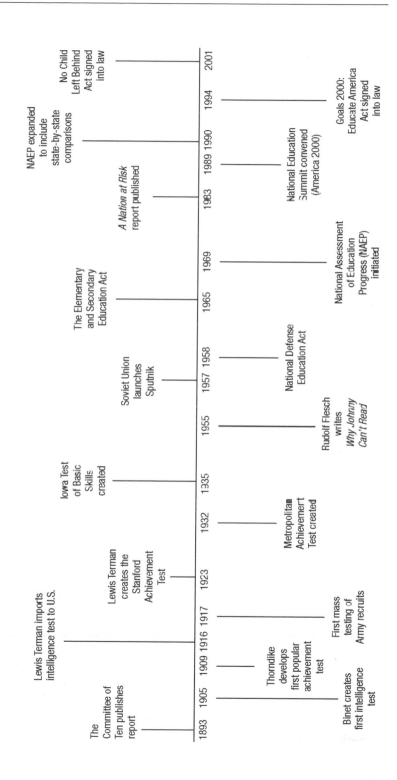

curriculum should reflect the needs of college-bound students as opposed to "terminal" students—that is, those who would not go on to college. The Committee of Ten acknowledged the differing needs of students who were college bound and those who were not, but ultimately recommended that both groups take an academic curriculum based almost entirely on a college preparatory format (Pulliam & Van Patten, 1998). In this way, academic achievement was made the cornerstone of U.S. education, a bias that continues to the present day.

Also significant to the early development of Academic Achievement Discourse was the creation and implementation of standardized testing programs in the United States in the early part of the 20th century. At the forefront of this movement was one of the world's first educational psychologists, Edward L. Thorndike. According to David Berliner (1993): "Thorndike promoted the belief that science and only science would save education. Indeed, he believed it would save all of society. His belief was that quantitative experiments were to be preferred over qualitative, clinical, or naturalistic observation" (p. 64). In 1909, Thorndike developed the first standardized achievement test popularly used in the public schools: the Thorndike Handwriting Scale. Another key event was the creation of the first intelligence test in 1905 by Alfred Binet. In 1916, Stanford professor Lewis Terman published a revised edition of the Binet-Simon Scale known as the Stanford-Binet intelligence test, and adopted German psychologist William Stern's suggestion to create a single intelligence quotient for the test. In this way, the I.Q. score was born. In May 1917, Terman and others developed the first mass intelligence tests given to millions of U.S. military recruits serving in World War I (see Gould, 1996). In 1919, the Rockefeller Foundation awarded Terman a grant to develop a national intelligence test for children. Within a year, 400,000 tests were available for use in public elementary schools. In 1923, Terman developed the Stanford Achievement Test, the first of several comprehensive national achievement tests, including the Metropolitan Achievement Test published in 1932 and the Iowa Test of Basic

Skills in 1935. These tests were given to tens of millions of school children over the next 80 years. Thorndike and Terman thereby unleashed the mass use of standardized tests that were to become the dynamic force behind Academic Achievement Discourse in the United States.

Fast forward to 1955, when an Austrian émigré named Rudolf Flesch published the national best-seller, *Why Johnny Can't Read,* which assailed the use of basal readers such as the Dick and Jane series and criticized the "whole word" or "look-say" method of reading instruction (Flesch, 1986). Flesch's book promoted the idea of phonics as the preferred method of teaching reading. As part of his critique, Flesch claimed that U.S. school children advanced more slowly than European school children in reading, and that the failure of public schools to educate children was a threat to democracy. Flesch thereby engaged in one of the first examples of Academic Achievement Discourse to be picked up by the newly established mass media empire, and it turned into a national debate on how to educate our children. Flesch articulated several assumptions of Academic Achievement Discourse in his crusade, including prioritizing reading over other school subjects, comparing U.S. students' academic performance to that of students in other countries, and connecting reading failure with a potential future event: the deterioration of democratic institutions.

These national concerns about the poor performance of U.S. school children were amplified considerably on October 4, 1957, when the Soviet Union launched Sputnik I into outer space. The next month, the picture of the inventor of the hydrogen bomb, U.S. scientist Edward Teller, appeared on the cover of *Time* magazine, and Teller warned in the accompanying article: "Many people are afraid we will be attacked by Russia. I am not free of such worry. But I do not think this is the most probable way in which they will defeat us. They will advance so fast in science and leave us so far behind that their way of doing things will be the way, and there will be nothing we can do about it" ("Knowledge Is Power," 1957).

Congress responded to Sputnik in 1958 by passing the National Defense Education Act, which authorized $887 million over four years for college loans, scholarships, equipment, and research in the areas of math, science, and foreign languages (Bruccoli & Layman, 1994). An important result of the Russian space effort and the U.S. response was that math and science education joined reading instruction as the most valued and most highly funded subjects in schools across the United States.

As part of President Johnson's War on Poverty in the socially conscious 1960s, Congress passed the Elementary and Secondary Education Act in 1965, which became the largest single act for K–12 education by the federal government ever instituted in the United States. It has provided billions of dollars of assistance annually over the past 40 years to poor schools, communities, and children, and has become the granddaddy of all subsequent federal programs in education, including Head Start, the Individuals with Disabilities Education Improvement Act (IDEA), and the No Child Left Behind Act. The effect of this law was to vastly expand the role of the federal government in education and also to expand the scope of state educational bureaucracies in administering federal funds.

Once the federal government had assumed a major role in administering funds to schools, it was only a short jump to the development of a national assessment system that could monitor the effectiveness of government intervention. In 1969, the National Assessment of Educational Progress, also known as "the Nation's Report Card," was first established with financial support provided by the Carnegie Foundation and other private sources, as well as by the federal government. The federal government later assumed full responsibility for its funding and administration (Vinovskis, 1998). The National Assessment of Educational Progress tested students ages 9, 13, and 17 in reading, mathematics, and science achievement. It was not long after this that the term "accountability" entered the discourse of educators. Wesleyan University professor Richard Ohmann (2000) explained:

In June 1970 "accountability" first showed up in the Education Index, the main general database for education, with reference to teaching. The Library of Congress introduced "educational accountability" as a subject heading two years later. A keyword search at the library I use (University of Massachusetts, Amherst) turned up 585 book titles, only 6 of them predating 1970 and none of those 6 about education. In 1970, *Every Kid a Winner: Accountability in Education,* by education professor Leon M. Lessinger, appeared; the book was soon characterized as the "bible of accountability." Over the next five years, dozens of books were published with titles such as *Accountability and Reading Instruction; Accountability and the Community College; Accountability for Educational Results; Accountability for Teachers and School Administrators.* . . . Accountability had abruptly become an established idea joined at the hip to education, a recognized field of study, a movement.

In the late 1970s, the "back to basics" movement, initially established to counter the "negative" effects (i.e., falling test scores) of the open education movement of the 1960s and early 1970s, moved the national education agenda even closer to engagement with academic skills and higher academic standards. Another key event in the history of Academic Achievement Discourse was initiated in 1981, when President Reagan and Secretary of Education Terrell Bell convened the National Commission on Excellence in Education to investigate the quality of education in America's schools. The commission's 1983 report, *A Nation at Risk,* excoriated U.S. schools for their mediocre performance and recommended, among other things, the establishment of a common core curriculum and national academic standards. It declared that "all, regardless of race or class or economic status, are entitled to a fair chance and to the tools for developing their individual powers of mind and spirit to the utmost" (National Commission on Excellence in Education, 1983, p. 1). Education historian Diane Ravitch (2003b) interpreted this phrase as follows:

Among educators, this message was translated to mean, "All children can learn." This earnest maxim repudiated the long-established practice of separating children into different programs on the basis of their likelihood of going to college. "All children can learn" changed the rules of the game in American education; it shifted the debate from discussions about access and resources to discussion about results. It was no longer enough to provide equal facilities; it became necessary to justify programs and expenditures on the basis of whether students made genuine gains. The rhetoric and philosophy of "all children can learn" had a large impact on education issues, as it became increasingly clear that educators needed not only to set higher expectations, but also to devise methods and incentives to get almost all students to learn more and to exert greater effort. After *Risk*, every state and school district scrutinized its standards and curricula, changed high school graduation requirements, and insisted that students take more courses in academic subjects. (p. 38)

The 1990s saw the enactment into law of many of the recommendations for academic excellence that had been gaining ground during the previous two decades. In 1989, President Bush convened the nation's governors for the first National Education Summit. The governors established six objectives for educational improvement (dubbed America 2000) that were to be reached by the year 2000, including improving high school graduation rates to 90 percent; ensuring that students in grades 4, 8, and 12 demonstrated competency in English, mathematics, science, history, and geography; and making the U.S. number one in the world in math and science achievement. A national agenda was finally being fashioned for U.S. students based on tougher academic requirements. In 1990, the National Assessment of Educational Progress began to include state-by-state testing (a move that was initially opposed in 1968 by several educational organizations that feared that the results would be misused), thereby providing a more sophisticated means of monitoring academic progress and a way to compare performances of the 50 states with regard to these new objectives. In 1994, President Clinton signed into law a version of America 2000 called the Goals 2000: Educate America Act, which established a commission to draw up national standards for academic achievement. That same year, Congress also passed the Improving America's School's

Act, which required the states to develop performance standards, create assessments that were aligned to those standards, and establish benchmarks for improvement (known as adequate yearly progress). Legislative activity in the 1990s thereby created the national framework that ultimately led to the crowning achievement of Academic Achievement Discourse, the No Child Left Behind Act.

Negative Consequences of Academic Achievement Discourse

At this point in the chapter, some readers may be thinking: "I don't understand. I've always believed that academic achievement is a good thing! Don't we want our students to work hard, learn a lot, get good grades, and make something of themselves in life?" My answer is: "Of course we do." The problem is that when the dialogue in education becomes limited to the narrow framework of grades, test scores, and scientifically based research, then a great deal of what education is about gets left behind. Moreover, the excessive concentration on developing uniform standards, implementing a rigorous curriculum, and raising test scores has several negative consequences that are creating more harm to students and teachers than benefits. What follows are some of the most serious negative consequences of Academic Achievement Discourse.

Negative Consequence #1: Academic Achievement Discourse results in a neglect of areas of the curriculum that are part of a well-rounded education students need in order to experience success and fulfillment in life.

Because the focus of Academic Achievement Discourse is on academics, vocational education, for example, is given less emphasis, even though many students will leave school and ultimately make their livelihood from vocational pursuits. Because the focus in academics is primarily on core academic subjects (reading, writing, mathematics, and science), those parts of the curriculum that are considered on the periphery (art, music, physical education, etc.) are neglected. A recent report commissioned by the Council for Basic Education, for example, found that the schools are becoming more committed to the core academic areas of reading, writing, mathematics, science, and secondary school social studies, and less committed to the arts, foreign languages, and elementary social studies, with the greatest erosion of the curriculum coming from schools with a high minority population (Von Zastrow & Janc, 2004).

Negative Consequence #2: Academic Achievement Discourse results in a neglect of positive instructional interventions that cannot be validated by scientifically based research data.

As noted above in the discussion of assumptions, Academic Achievement Discourse favors the adoption of educational programs that can be measured through random controlled trials and other so-called rigorous research methods. Thus, educational techniques and strategies that might work well for individual students, that are used by creative teachers on the spur of the moment to meet a specific teaching challenge, or that are best measured through qualitative research methods, cannot be considered valid because these approaches cannot be measured through random controlled trials or similar quantitative methods. It appears that the programs most likely to receive support and validation from scientifically based research data are those that actually look very much like the tests that are going to be used to validate them. Thus, for example, Direct Instruction (DI) has proved to be one of the instructional models with the greatest support from scientifically based research data. With DI, the teacher delivers carefully scripted lesson plans to students that break material down into small segments that need to be mastered before students move on. The use of worksheets containing problems that are similar to those that will be on the validating achievement tests suggests that

Direct Instruction succeeds because it constitutes scripted preparation for those very same validating research instruments.

Instructional approaches that may result in students developing positive attitudes, life skills, or complex concepts that are not reflected in achievement test results will be less likely to receive funding and support. Reading expert Gerald Coles (2003), for example, commenting on the Reading First provisions of the NCLB Act, wrote: "With 'Reading First' a McCarthyist blacklist has emerged. Applicants for the legislation's funds have quickly learned which blacklisted concepts, terminology, publications, and scholars to avoid. Educators . . . feel compelled to comply because educational funding is scarce" (para. 9).

Negative Consequence #3: Academic Achievement Discourse encourages teaching to the test.

Because achievement tests are made the sole or primary measure of student and school improvement in Academic Achievement Discourse, teachers turn their attention toward test preparation skills and away from learning for its own sake. The independent research body FairTest (2004) concluded: "'Teaching to the test' narrows the curriculum and forces teachers and students to concentrate on memorizing isolated facts" (p. 1). Instead of creating learning environments in which students are free to explore new concepts and problems in creative and unpredictable ways, students must now go through learning experiences that are essentially replicas of test conditions. One New York teacher reported: "'We start preparing them in September. When I go through a lesson, I always connect it to what's in the exam. We know there's always letter-writing, so we give more of that. We know there's nonfiction, so we make sure we do it before the test.' When she gives a writing assignment, she now sets a timer for 10 minutes to simulate testing conditions" (Winerip, 2005, p. B11). Increasingly, school districts are employing the services of test preparation consultants who can help coach teachers in ways to boost test scores.

Negative Consequence #4: Academic Achievement Discourse encourages student cheating and plagiarism.

Because success in school is tied so heavily to just a few high-stakes tests given during the year, students use test-taking strategies that are not included as part of the test-preparation program. That is, they learn to cheat and plagiarize. In a survey conducted by Who's Who Among American High School Students, 80 percent of these high-achieving scholars said that they had cheated in school at least once. "Crib sheets and copying answers are nothing new," observed Carolyn Kleiner and Mary Lord (1999). "What's changed, experts maintain, is the scope of the problem: the technology that opens new avenues to cheat, students' boldness in using it, and the erosion of conscience at every level of education" (p. 54).

Negative Consequence #5: Academic Achievement Discourse encourages manipulation of test results by teachers and administrators.

Because teachers, administrators, and state education officials are pressured into producing high test results to meet state and federal requirements, they begin creatively massaging the statistics and in some cases engage in outright cheating themselves. Educational statisticians now speak regularly of "the Lake Wobegon" effect (based on Garrison Keillor's mythical town of Lake Wobegon, "where all the children are above average"), a situation in which all states report above-average achievement data, even though this is statistically impossible. In the Houston school system, dropouts were conveniently left out of a report on improved Houston achievement test results. "The Houston school district reported a citywide dropout rate of 1.5 percent. But educators and experts *60 Minutes* [the CBS television news program] checked with put Houston's true dropout rate somewhere between 25 and 50 percent" (CBS News, 2004, para. 14). In Illinois, a study by economics professor Steven Leavitt suggested that serious cases of teacher or principal cheating occurred in 5 percent of elementary classrooms in the Chicago School District (Leavitt & Dubner, 2005).

Negative Consequence #6: Academic Achievement Discourse encourages the student use of illegal substances as performance aids.

In order to cope with the mandate of tougher and more rigorous courses and school requirements, students are increasingly turning to stimulant drugs and other performance enhancers to help them stay alert while doing their homework or studying for an exam. In some cases, students who have been legitimately prescribed Ritalin, Adderall, or other psychostimulants for ADD/ADHD are giving or selling them to their peers for an "academic boost." "It's like mental steroids," said Becky Beacom, manager of health education at the Palo Alto [California] Medical Foundation. "Students think they need that extra edge to get into college." Seven percent of 1,304 Palo Alto high school students surveyed said they had used such substances without a prescription at least once. "'It's like caffeine or Red Bull,' said a Los Altos [California] high school senior who said his friend gives him Adderall to help him focus on finals or major papers. 'It's like any other pick-me-up'" (Patel, 2005). Unfortunately, these drugs come with dangers—especially to those for whom the drug has not been prescribed—including addiction, tics, and in rare instances, psychoses.

Negative Consequence #7: Academic Achievement Discourse transfers control of the curriculum away from educators in the classroom and toward the organizations that set the standards and exams.

Educators are the experts in teaching and learning, not politicians, government officials, or standardized test companies. Unfortunately, the increasing emphasis on using achievement tests to measure school improvement means that the power to control the structure and flow of learning is being handed over to bureaucrats who have little understanding of the process of teaching and learning. One middle school teacher who was attempting to implement an integrated curriculum in his school registered his shock when told that the school would have to spend less instructional time on social studies and science in the curriculum.

> As a social studies teacher and member of an 8th grade interdisciplinary team, I could not believe what I was hearing. Yet, as the principal proceeded to explain to our team why we needed to add more time to English and mathematics at the expense of social studies and science, I could begrudgingly understand her logic: A high percentage of our students had failed previous administrations of our state's high-stakes test, the Massachusetts Comprehensive Assessment System (MCAS) . . . all students must pass the English and mathematics sections of the MCAS as a requirement for high school graduation. Therefore, more instructional time should be devoted to English and mathematics, and less instructional time should be spent on subjects such as social studies and science that are tested but do not have a MCAS passing score requirement for high school graduation. (Vogler, 2003, p. 5)

Negative Consequence #8: Academic Achievement Discourse produces harmful levels of stress in teachers and students.

As students are subjected to more and more pressure from harder course requirements, more homework, and test anxiety, those who are particularly vulnerable to stress develop stress-related symptoms such as sleep disturbances, irritability, difficulty concentrating, headaches or stomachaches, aggressiveness, and learning problems. As one Texas teacher says of her state's high-stakes test, the Texas Assessment of Knowledge and Skills (TAKS): "Practice TAKS tests are a weekly, if not daily, occurrence. I've seen 8-year-olds suffering from sleep deprivation due to stress and test anxiety" (Reyher, 2005, para. 5). Stanford professor Denis Clark Pope (2003) followed several high-achieving high school students and discovered the same thing: "To keep up her grades, Eve sleeps just two or three hours a night and lives in a constant state of stress. Kevin faces anxiety and frustration as he attempts to balance the high expectations of his father with his own desire 'to have a life' outside of school. . . . Both Teresa and Roberto resort to drastic actions when they worry they will not maintain the grades they need for future careers" (p. 3).

Forced to teach under conditions not of their own choosing and faced with sanctions for noncompliance with tougher requirements, teachers also undergo stress symptoms, and many eventually burn out and leave teaching. A 1996 survey by the National Education Association (Delisio, 2001) revealed that the majority of teachers who leave the profession do so because of stress-related factors. "I think stress levels [among teachers] are very high because expectations are high and demands are much higher," said Albert Madden, a guidance counselor at Stevens Elementary School in Williamsport, Pennsylvania. "Part of the reason teachers experience burn-out symptoms is they do care so much and there is so much they can't control" (Delisio, 2001, para. 4).

Negative Consequence #9: Academic Achievement Discourse increases the chances that students will be retained from year to year and drop out before graduation.

Many students who are already in academic difficulty find their problems multiplied with the addition of more reading assignments, homework, and test pressure. As tests increasingly determine who can move on to the next grade level and eventually graduate, more and more students are being retained from grade to grade. As frustration mounts, there is increasing motivation for these individuals to drop out of school entirely. A recent Arizona State University study of the high-stakes pressures associated with the No Child Left Behind Act concluded that increases in testing pressures are *not* associated with improved academic achievement, but *are* associated with increased retention and dropout rates (Nichols, Glass, & Berliner, 2005). Former teacher and education critic Susan Ohanian pointed to research findings on the relationship between retention and dropouts: "Hold ten students back a grade and only three will be around on graduation day; hold those students back twice and none will complete school. None. And African-American and Latino students are retained at twice the rate of white students" (Ohanian, 2003, p. 29).

Negative Consequence #10: Academic Achievement Discourse fails to take into consideration individual differences in cultural backgrounds, learning styles and rates, and other crucial factors in the lives of real children.

Academic Achievement Discourse favors a one-size-fits-all mentality when fashioning curricula, standards, and test requirements. This accords well with a belief in equity (all children can learn), but fails to consider the vast differences in students' backgrounds, preparedness for learning, social and emotional growth, learning abilities and difficulties, temperament, interests, and preferences. A Portland, Oregon, teacher reflected on how lock-step academic requirements failed to recognize the unique needs of her students:

> Farida came to Roosevelt from a refugee camp in East Africa. Her heart is full of the deaths she witnessed—family members lined up and shot. She had never held a pen or pencil before coming to Roosevelt at age 15. As a newcomer to the United States, Farida was forced to take tests in English, a language she only just began learning three years ago. She needs time to recover, to learn to read and to write. She needs time. . . . Michael, at 17, reads at a 4th-grade level. Every paragraph holds undecipherable mysteries for his struggling mind. No wonder he gave up on the state standardized reading test, the test he has now tried and failed three times. (Ambrosio, 2003, para. 13–14)

Negative Consequence #11: Academic Achievement Discourse undercuts the intrinsic value of learning for its own sake.

Because Academic Achievement Discourse employs learning activities in the classroom that are designed to improve scores on academic achievement tests, the whole process of learning becomes devalued; students no longer learn simply for the joy of it but in order to obtain higher grades and test scores. As Kohn (1999) and others have pointed out, when students engage in classroom activities in order to be rewarded for them (with praise, gold stars, good grades, or high test scores), their intrinsic motivation suffers. Since intrinsic motivation is, arguably, the most important quality to be nurtured in the course of a child's education, the undermining of the joy of learning may be one of the most tragic unseen consequences of Academic Achievement Discourse (see, for example, Armstrong, 1991, 1998).

Negative Consequence #12: Academic Achievement Discourse results in the institution of developmentally inappropriate practices in the schools.

As a result of the focus on high standards, a tougher curriculum, and high-stakes tests, educators have begun to prepare students for the rigors of academia at earlier and earlier ages. Practices previously considered developmentally appropriate for 1st graders have now been pushed back to kindergarten. Increasingly, early childhood education is being invaded by homework, seat work, worksheets, computer time, a longer school day, less time for recess, and other developmentally inappropriate practices. (See Chapter 3 for a fuller discussion.) At the Malaika Early Learning Center in Milwaukee, Wisconsin, young children attend school from 9:00 a.m. to 3:15 p.m. "Twenty years ago, people would have said, 'That's too much for a 4-year-old; we are pushing them too hard,'" Keona Jones, the director of the center, said. "Now we understand that to close the achievement gap, we have to have more minutes of instructional time" (Carr, 2004, para. 44).

   In addition to impairing the quality of early childhood education programs, Academic Achievement Discourse has also resulted in an increase in the incidence of developmentally inappropriate practices at *all* levels of schooling, from preschool to high school. It will be the job of the rest of this book to examine exactly how this damage has occurred and detail what needs to be done to make sure that children and adolescents are educated not according to political agendas and testing timetables but according to their own natural patterns of growth and development. To begin this examination, we turn in the next chapter to an exploration of an alternative form of educational discourse, Human Development Discourse, which occurs far less frequently than it did in decades past but needs to be quickly resuscitated if our schools and our culture are going to have a chance of retaining their humanity.

For Further Study

1. How often do you and your colleagues engage in Academic Achievement Discourse? Look at the following list of key words and phrases in Academic Achievement Discourse and notice during a typical school day how often these words are used in conversations or written communications with students, teachers, administrators, or parents.

Academic success or failure
Acceleration
Accountability
Adequate yearly (or sufficient)
   progress
Alignment (of curriculum) to
   standards
Annual assessments
Below or above grade level
Benchmarks
Calibrate
Closing the achievement gap
Consequences
Content
Data
Diagnostic instruments
Effectiveness
Excellence

Failure
Falling behind
Goals
High (or low) expectations
High-stakes tests
Implementation
Improvement
Low- or high-performing
   schools
Low- or high-performing
   students
Mandates
Mastery
Minimum requirements
Normative
Norms
Objectives
Outcomes

Percentiles	Rigorous curriculum
Performance	Rubrics
Progress	Sanctions
Raising the bar	Scientifically based research
Readiness	Standards
Remediation	Targets
Rewards	

Are there particular contexts in which these words are used more often (e.g., staff meetings, individualized education plan meetings, pre-test classroom situations)? Keep a one-day written record of every time a word or phrase on this list appears in your conversations or in communications that you've written or read. Discuss the results with colleagues. Add any words or phrases not found on the list that you believe also constitute a part of Academic Achievement Discourse.

2. Discuss with your colleagues which particular negative consequences of Academic Achievement Discourse described in this chapter apply most to your own school setting. Give concrete examples from your school day. What other negative consequences not specifically mentioned in this chapter seem to occur in your school setting as a result of Academic Achievement Discourse?

3. In your opinion, do the positive consequences of Academic Achievement Discourse outweigh the negative consequences, or vice versa? Discuss with colleagues the pluses and minuses of increased national emphasis on testing, a rigorous curriculum, uniform standards, No Child Left Behind, graduation requirements, and other similar educational trends. Do you see your own school moving closer to or farther away from these kinds of practices?

4. Investigate the history of Academic Achievement Discourse by looking up the history of education in an encyclopedia, online search engine, or other reference guide. Explore the roots of Academic Achievement Discourse in the development of Western civilization (e.g., during the Enlightenment, in the medieval university system, in ancient Rome and Greece).

2

Human Development
Discourse

In the 20 years that I've spent as a teacher trainer, there is one question that has been asked more than any other. It goes something like this: "Yes, Dr. Armstrong, what you have to say is very interesting about these new teaching practices, but what does the research say about how this will raise academic achievement levels in students?" Naturally, I try to give them what they have asked for and cite various studies and experiments that I hope will placate their need for information. However, I get frustrated with the frequency of this question and, instead of regurgitating research data, I often ask them a question of my own: "How many of you went into the teaching profession because you wanted to boost test scores?" In the 20 years that I have been presenting seminars and workshops, not one teacher has ever raised his or her hand. Then I ask another question: "How many of you went into the teaching profession because you wanted to help kids reach their full potential?" Invariably, most of the teachers' hands go up.

This presents an interesting dilemma. On the one hand, teachers seem to be reluctant to adopt educational reforms unless they are assured that these changes will result in higher academic achievement results. Another way of putting this is that when push comes to shove, teachers engage in Academic Achievement Discourse. And yet, when asked a question that attempts to plumb the depths of their own belief systems about learning ("What led you to become a teacher in the first place?"), *none* of them indicate that improving hard data in academic achievement was the motivating force. Instead, teachers talk about "softer" things such as inspiring children, unlocking potential, nurturing the development of young lives, making a difference in the lives of students, and ensuring student success in life. Teachers are saying that *these* are the things that really matter as far as educating the next generation is concerned.

When teachers and other educators talk in this way, they are engaging in a very different kind of conversation from that of Academic Achievement Discourse. They are participating in what I call Human Development Discourse. In this chapter, I'll describe the core assumptions of Human Development Discourse, give a history of the development of this discourse in education, and finally, outline what I see as several positive consequences of engaging in this discourse at a fundamentally deep level in the schools. I say "at a fundamentally deep level" because some individuals and institutions engage in Human Development Discourse at a very superficial level to mask the fact that they are actually engaging in Academic Achievement Discourse. For example, in the last chapter, we noted that the influential 1983 report *A Nation at Risk* included the following opening sentence: "All, regardless of race or class or economic status, are entitled to a fair chance and to the tools for developing their individual powers of mind and spirit to the utmost" (National Commission on Excellence in Education, 1983, p. 1). As we will see in this chapter, the phrase "developing their individual powers of mind and spirit to the utmost" is a good example of Human Development Discourse. And yet *A Nation at Risk* was fundamentally a document that strongly favored tougher high school graduation requirements, more academic courses (English, math, science, computer science, social science), more "rigorous and measurable standards," and more time spent on coursework and study. All of these recommendations are key components of Academic Achievement Discourse.

Similarly, in the preamble to the 2001 No Child Left Behind Act, President George W. Bush wrote: "Taken together, these reforms express my deep belief in our public schools and their mission to build the mind and character of every child, from every background, in every part of America" (U.S. Department of Education, 2002, p. 2). In using the phrase "to build the mind and character of every child," President Bush is gesturing toward Human Development Discourse. And yet the law's real teeth are primarily measures that enforce, through sanctions, the boosting of academic achievement test scores. When we listen to Human Development Discourse going on in educational circles, we should train ourselves to distinguish between instances in which it is being used as window dressing to hide another kind of discourse or agenda, and instances in which it is being used to fundamentally address all levels of the educational process, from research and assessment to instruction and school leadership.

Human Development Discourse: A Definition

If we start with the first word in this discourse—"human"—we can discover a great deal about its definition, especially when it is counterpoised against the first word in Academic Achievement Discourse—"academic." We learn right away that the most important thing about this discourse is that it places the greatest emphasis on *human beings* rather than on *academics.* Thus, Human Development Discourse has a substantially wider perspective than Academic Achievement Discourse. "Academics" represents something that is not living and that is objective and finite. On the other hand, "human" represents an entity that is living, subjective, and arguably infinite. If we were to fully define the world of academics (a dead world of content), eventually we would reach a point where we had covered every aspect of it. On the other hand, in defining "human," it's very probable that we would never come to an end in our discussions of what it means to be human. "Academics" are *out there* in the form of books, tests, lectures, requirements, syllabi, and so forth. "Human" is *in here*—it is *ourselves* that we're talking about. The discourse and the one who engages in the discourse are the same entity. Given the fact that we're talking about ourselves in this discourse, we'd have to conclude that there is far more significance, and far more at stake, in engaging in Human Development Discourse than in Academic Achievement Discourse.

The second word of each discourse is similarly revealing. In Human Development Discourse, we learn that what's most important is the *development* of humans. The word "develop" is etymologically related to an earlier English word "*disvelop*," a Provençal word, "*desvolopar*," and a modern Italian word "*sviluppare*," which hold the meanings of "unwrapping," "unrolling," "unfolding," "disentangling," and "ridding free" (Simpson & Weiner, 1991, p. 423). Thus, what seem to be the themes of Human Development Discourse are the unrolling or unfolding of the human, as well as the sense of disentangling, ridding, or freeing the human from encumbrances, complications, or obstacles.

On the other hand, *achievement* is related to the French phrase "*à chief (venir)*," which goes back to the Latin "*ad caput venire*," which means "to bring to a head" or "to finish" (Simpson & Weiner, 1991, p. 12). The word "development" suggests an ongoing process, something that is happening over time. Something that is human is coming into being or being freed. The word "achievement" is quite different in meaning. It is not about a process over time but about the *end result*. It's as if "achievement" were saying: "Don't bother me with what has already happened, or is happening right now, just wrap it up, bring it to an end, finish it up. Be done with it! Caput!" Human Development Discourse is interested in the whole story *as it unfolds*. Academic Achievement Discourse is interested in going to the last page and finding out if the butler did it! (See Figure 2.1 for a comparison of key characteristics of the two discourses.)

Although it may seem to some that I'm going into needless detail in spelling out these word origins, I believe that these underlying differences in word etymologies underscore powerful differences that exist between each of these two types of educational discourse. A good working definition of Human Development

Figure 2.1

Comparing Characteristics of Academic Achievement Discourse and Human Development Discourse

Context	Approach	
	Academic Achievement Discourse	Human Development Discourse
Intellectual Tradition	positivism	humanism
Temporal Orientation	future-oriented	past-present-future-oriented
Primary Approach to Research	quantitative	qualitative
Primary Method of Student Assessment	standardized testing	naturalistic observation and documentation
Power Structure	top-down mandates	ideas spread at grassroots level
Most Valued Aspect of Learning	end product	the process from beginning to end
Method of Measuring Student Progress	normative	ipsative
Most Important Thing to Be Taught	academic skills	how to live as a whole human being
Most Important Party to Learning	institutions (schools, districts, states)	individual human beings
Most Important Role of Teachers	to meet institutional mandates	to inspire in students a passion for learning
Bases Its Claims for Validity On	scientifically based research	the richness of human experience
Most Important Subjects in School	reading, math, science	life skills, the arts, vocational education, the humanities, the sciences, and the connections between them
Bottom Line	high test scores, money	maturity, happiness

Discourse as used in education might be "the totality of speech acts and written communications that view the purpose of education primarily in terms of supporting, encouraging, and facilitating a student's growth as a whole human being, including his or her cognitive, emotional, social, ethical, creative, and spiritual unfoldment." In what follows, I counterpoise each assumption of Academic Achievement Discourse described in the last chapter with a corresponding assumption for Human Development Discourse.

Assumption #1: Becoming *a whole human being* is the most important aspect of learning.

Academic Achievement Discourse tends to narrow the aims of education to just the successful acquisition of academic content and skills. On the other hand, Human Development Discourse comes closer to capturing the original meaning of the word "education," which goes back to the Latin word "*educare*": "to bring forth." The word "education" is also etymologically related to the word "educe," which means "to bring out, elicit, develop, from a condition of latent, rudimentary or merely potential existence" (Simpson & Weiner, 1991, p. 496). Thus we discover that, at heart, education is actually the means of facilitating human development. Nowhere in the definition of education do we see a reference to "boosting test scores." Stanford Professor of Education Nel Noddings (2005) has pointed out that the history of American education is rooted in this sense of the development of the whole person. She noted, for example, that Thomas Jefferson included in his *1818 Report of the Commissioners for the University of Virginia* a list of educational goals that included morals, understanding duties to neighbors and country, knowledge of rights, and intelligence and faithfulness in social relations. In addition, the National Education Association, in its 1918 report *Cardinal Principles of Secondary Education*, detailed seven aims of education, including health, command of the fundamental processes, worthy home membership, vocation, citizenship, worthy use of leisure, and ethical character. Since that time, many other educators and psychologists have engaged in research and created theories and programs designed to describe and *draw forth* through education many aspects of what it means to develop as a human being cognitively, affectively, socially, morally, and spiritually. The work of many of these thinkers will be described in the next section of this chapter.

Assumption #2: Evaluating the growth of a whole human being is a meaningful, ongoing, and *qualitative* process that itself involves human growth.

The primary means of measurement or evaluation of student improvement in Academic Achievement Discourse is the use of standardized achievement tests, which are themselves not learning experiences but rather artificial environments created through a collaboration of test manufacturers, educational researchers, and educators. These artificial "events" occur at specific moments in time that are *interruptions* in the actual experiences of learning. In other words, students must *stop learning* and engage in testing—for a period of 45 minutes or 2 hours or an entire day or week—in order for educators to measure what they've learned during a previous period of instruction. Human Development Discourse, on the other hand, is concerned with measuring learning growth *in the midst of the learning experience itself*. Foremost among the approaches used to assess learning in Human Development Discourse is the recording of the actual learning experiences of each student over time. This includes what a student has said, drawn, written, felt, sung, experimented with, thought about (to the extent that it can be outwardly shown), demonstrated, or otherwise expressed in some meaningful fashion within a real learning context. The assessment itself serves as a learning experience for the student. For example, a student might sit down with a teacher and discuss 20 samples of her poetry written from September to December, or view videotapes of her interaction with classmates made during the beginning and end of a semester. Thus students learn more about themselves as a result of the process of assessment. This process provides vivid and tangible evidence of learning that is not possible to obtain through letter grades and test scores.

Assumption #3: Human Development Discourse favors a curriculum that is *flexible*, that is *individualized*, and that gives students *meaningful choices*.

Rather than the one-size-fits-all mentality of Academic Achievement Discourse, which seeks to run students through a standardized academic maze on their way to school success, Human Development Discourse seeks to regard each individual student as a unique human being with his or her own particular way of negotiating the developmental challenges of life. Thus, there is a respect for each student's particular style and rate of learning, as well as an appreciation for the varied interests, aspirations, capacities, obstacles, temperaments, and backgrounds that serve as the framework within which each person grows. Rather than insisting upon the student's mastery of a given body of information, Human Development Discourse is much more concerned with tailoring the curriculum around the specific needs of the student. Instead of mandating what all students must learn, Human Development Discourse involves creating learning environments that let a student make meaningful choices about what he will learn in the course of his school experiences to help develop into his own unique versions of a whole human being.

Assumption #4: Human Development Discourse is interested in the *past*, *present*, and *future* of every student.

While Academic Achievement Discourse places a premium on the *future* (e.g., preparing every student for the challenges of the 21st century), Human Development Discourse is concerned with the entire trajectory over time of students' development, from their earliest experiences in childhood to their ultimate expressions of maturity in adulthood. Concern is given, for example, to traumatic experiences that may have occurred in the life of a student during infancy or early childhood that might have created obstacles to growth and learning in the present. Human Development Discourse speaks of viable options to facilitate development, including the provision of a safe learning environment, the building of trust in the learning relationship, and the use of other therapeutic approaches to foster optimal growth. Similarly, Human Development Discourse goes beyond seeing success in the future only in terms of college, graduate school, and a lucrative, powerful, or prestigious job. Although these goals may be part of successful development for some students, Human Development Discourse seeks to nurture a student's abilities so that her future may include successful relationships with others, meaningful service to the community, emotional maturity, ethical behavior, and a passion for learning, among many other nonacademic goals. Most importantly, Human Development Discourse views the present teachable moment as the single best opportunity for healing a student's early educational wounding and inspiring positive aspirations toward the future.

Assumption #5: Human Development Discourse is *ipsative* in nature.

Most educators are familiar with the word "normative" as a testing term. This word refers to the process of comparing a student's academic performance on a standardized achievement test with a group of students who took the test under similar circumstances at some point in the past. The test results of the original student group are taken as the norm. In other words, this group is considered to represent "normal" behavior on the test, against which all future students are to be compared. Human Development Discourse, on the other hand, is much more involved in discussions of "ipsative" growth. "Ipsative" is a word that is generally not commonly used, or even known, in many educational circles. This itself is a testimony to the dominance of Academic Achievement Discourse in education. "Ipsative" means "from the self," and in the context of assessment in education it means comparing a person's present performance to the person's prior performances. We see this approach to assessment used most often in the arena of sports (e.g., "I increased my long jump distance 6 inches in the past four months!"). Because Human Development Discourse is concerned with individual human development, it views the ipsative approach as the most natural way to measure human growth and learning. At the beginning of the year, let's say, a student couldn't read *The Cat in the Hat,* do a pull-up, draw a picture of a person, use the phrase "Excuse me!" when bumping into somebody, or give a word to how he was feeling inside. At the end of the year he could do all of those things. Yet he received *D* grades and scored at a 30 percent level on achievement tests at the beginning and end of the year. From an Academic Achievement Discourse perspective, he's a normative failure. From a Human Development Discourse point of view, he's an ipsative success.

Assumption #6: Human Development Discourse bases its claims for validity on the richness of human experience.

Those who speak Academic Achievement Discourse pride themselves on the fact that their position is firmly established in scientifically based research data. They discount the efforts of those who use merely "anecdotal" information in their research. This attitude reveals a fundamental difference between Academic Achievement Discourse and Human Development Discourse in what kind of knowledge is most valued regarding a student. As we noted in the last chapter, Academic Achievement Discourse places greatest value on quantitative data (e.g., percentiles, stanines, correlation coefficients). Human Development Discourse, on the other hand, places greatest value on qualitative information: what a student does or experiences in a meaningful learning context. From the Academic Achievement Discourse standpoint, this information is regarded as inferior because it is considered fuzzy, inconsistent, and subjective. From a Human Development Discourse perspective, on the other hand, quantitative data is usually considered inferior as a basis for claims of validity because it is artificial, misleading, and detached from human experience.

We can view these two discourses against the broad background of the Western philosophical tradition. Academic Achievement Discourse is rooted in the tradition of "positivism," a belief that truth can only be found in objective scientific evidence. Forms of this approach are traceable to Greek philosophers such as Aristotle (trans. 1958) and Epicurus (trans. 1994), but this position had its real birth during the scientific discoveries of the 17th century (see, for example, Galileo, 1632/2001), and the 18th-century philosophical movement of the Enlightenment when philosophers such as La Mettrie (1748/1994), Locke (1690/1994), and later Auguste Comte (1830/1988) (with whom the term is most closely associated) argued that the empirical approach in science should be the basis of all human inquiry.

Human Development Discourse, on the other hand, is rooted in the tradition of humanism, that stream of philosophical thought that affirms the dignity and worth of all people. Forms of this intellectual tradition can be traced back to Greek thinkers such as Plato (trans. 1986), with his deep appreciation of the good, the true, and the beautiful, and emerged more recently during the 13th- to 16th-century Renaissance, when Western thinkers began to show a renewed interest in human rather than theological matters as revealed in art, poetry, architecture, and other fields of study (Ross & McLaughlin, 1977). The early 19th-century Romantic period (which in some respects was a counterreaction to the rational Enlightenment) saw a further expansion of humanistic themes, with its emphasis on the emotions, the imagination, and individual creative development as evidenced in the thinking of Rousseau (1781/1953), Goethe (1774/1989), and the Romantic poets (Auden & Pearson, 1977). In the 20th century, the philosophical school of phenomenology (see, for example, Husserl, 1970), which believes that truth can best be discovered in subjective human experience, and the school of existentialism (Kaufmann, 1988), which places a premium on affirmative individual human choice made in the midst of authoritarian belief systems or in the absence of *any* system to guide human conduct, served as additional philosophical foundations for Human Development Discourse. The point to be made here is that Human Development Discourse claims to validity are not *inferior* to Academic Achievement Discourse claims but are simply rooted in *a different intellectual tradition.*

Similarly, the research methods used in Human Development Discourse are not inferior to the scientifically based research methodologies of Academic Achievement Discourse. Rather, they are rooted in a humanist tradition. Research approaches that are congruent with Human Development Discourse and that can be used to explore the value of educational programs and methods include individual case studies, self-reports, phenomenologically based studies of student learning, hermeneutic interpretations of student work, heuristic studies, anthropological participant observation, ethnographic field studies, and qualitative action-based research, among many other qualitative approaches (see, for example, Bogdan & Bicklen, 1998; Denzin & Lincoln, 2005; LeCompte & Preissle, 1993; Merriam, 1998). Finally, it should be mentioned that Human Development Discourse claims to validity are frequently based on the commonsense experience of the actual participants in learning, and Academic Achievement Discourse claims are usually based on abstract data given by a remote expert.

To illustrate this dichotomy, I'd like to tell a story that has its origins in the Middle East. A man went to a friend's house to borrow his donkey. The friend answered the door and said that he was sorry but that he had lent his donkey out for the day. As the man was leaving the house, he heard the donkey braying in the back yard. He rushed back to the house and knocked on the door. The friend opened the door, and the man said, "I thought you lent your donkey out for the day!" The friend said, "Yes, I did." The man said, "But I can hear the donkey braying in the back yard!" The friend replied, "Who are you going to believe, the donkey or me?" (A version of this story can be found in Shah, 1993, p. 62.) Educators who use Human Development Discourse trust the evidence in front of their eyes—the "aha!" excitement of a child who just learned how a flower grows, the courage of a child's efforts to learn how to read in the midst of poverty, the transcendent glow in a child's eyes after making an art object. These intangibles—typically discounted in Academic Achievement Discourse—provide the real "data" that marks the development of a human being.

Assumption #7: Human Development Discourse generally takes place as part of a *grassroots effort* on the part of practitioners (e.g., teachers) inspired by individual creative thinkers in education and psychology.

In the last chapter, we noted that Academic Achievement Discourse occurs in a top-down fashion, which means that people with more power (politicians, administrators, researchers) impose their policies on people with less power (teachers and students). In contrast, Human Development Discourse is *egalitarian* in nature, involving administrators, teachers, and students in sharing knowledge and learning in an atmosphere of trust and synergy. It is not without its own power structure, of course, but generally it is the power of ideas and not politicians that is important here. Human Development Discourse often begins when a highly creative thinker—a Jean-Jacques Rousseau, Maria Montessori, Rudolf Steiner, John Dewey, or Jean Piaget, for example—shares his or her thoughts about how children grow and learn. This might be expressed in the form of a book (e.g., Rousseau's *Emile*), an experimental school (e.g., John Dewey's University of Chicago Lab School), or an educational program (e.g., the Montessori Method). From these beginnings, teachers are inspired to continue the discourse at a grassroots level by starting their own schools, writing their own books, creating their own programs, or in other ways making educational miracles happen with students. In this manner,

Human Development Discourse spreads its messages and meanings about human growth and learning throughout the world.

Assumption #8: The bottom line in Human Development Discourse is *happiness*.

One can, of course, think of many possibilities for the highest goals of education and human development: wisdom, integrity, creativity, self-actualization, character, open-mindedness, generosity, individuality, spirituality, and more. However, I feel that the quality of *happiness* comes closest to defining the bottom line of Human Development Discourse. I am not speaking here of happiness as a subjective emotional state. A child may be happy while eating some candy, but this kind of happiness will vanish in the next moment. Rather, I mean it much more in the sense that philosopher and Roman Emperor Marcus Aurelius did when he wrote: "The happiness and unhappiness of the rational, social animal depends not on what he feels but on what he does; just as his virtue and vice consist not in feeling but in doing" (Bartlett, 1919, p. 941). Happiness comes from deeds, not words, and from living life to its fullest. Similarly, happiness is not dependent on material wealth or outward achievements. In this respect it differs dramatically from the bottom line of Academic Achievement Discourse: money. As American educator and clergyman Henry van Dyke said, "Happiness is inward, and not outward; and so, it does not depend on what we have, but on what we are." The ultimate aim of Human Development Discourse is to facilitate the growth of a whole human being, one who despite obstacles and challenges is able to find deep satisfaction in the events of life. As Nel Noddings (2005) pointed out, "Great thinkers have associated happiness with such qualities as a rich intellectual life, rewarding human relationships, love of home and place, sound character, good parenting, spirituality, and a job that one loves" (p. 10). When these things are matched up against good test scores and a big bank account, there really is no contest.

A History of Human Development Discourse in Education

As we noted earlier in this chapter, the roots of Human Development Discourse can be found in a number of philosophical traditions, from Greek times to the present day. In this section, I'd like to provide a more specific account of how Human Development Discourse has evolved in education over the years (see Figure 2.2). Perhaps the earliest indications of Human Development Discourse at work in the Western world occur in Plato's *Republic*, where Socrates uses the dialectic method of inquiry to help some of his interlocutors advance one notch up the hierarchy of Bronze, Silver, and Gold personality types that were regarded by Socrates as generally fixed at birth (Segrue, 1995). In modern times, the 17th-century Czech educator John Amos Comenius (Jan Amos Komensky) is frequently credited with being the first thinker to regard education as a developmental process that begins in the earliest days of childhood and continues throughout one's life. Comenius created his educational philosophy in part from observing the processes of nature at work. He wrote: "Development comes from within. Nature compels nothing to advance that is not driven forward by its own mature strength" (as cited in LeBar, 1987, p. 19). He proceeded in his educational reforms to work *with* the forces of nature, rather than against them.

The 18th-century philosopher Jean-Jacques Rousseau took this natural approach in education to a higher level with the publication of his book *Emile,* which can be seen as the real initiator of Human Development Discourse in contemporary education. In this book, Rousseau described the ideal education of a boy named Emile (and later, a girl named Sophie), and he emphasized that children are born with the natural inclination to learn and that a proper education should respect the child's instincts to grow and should shelter the child from societal restrictions. In addressing mothers, Rousseau wrote: "It is to you that I address myself, tender and foresighted mother, who are capable of keeping the nascent shrub

Figure 2.2

Key Events in the History of Human Development Discourse

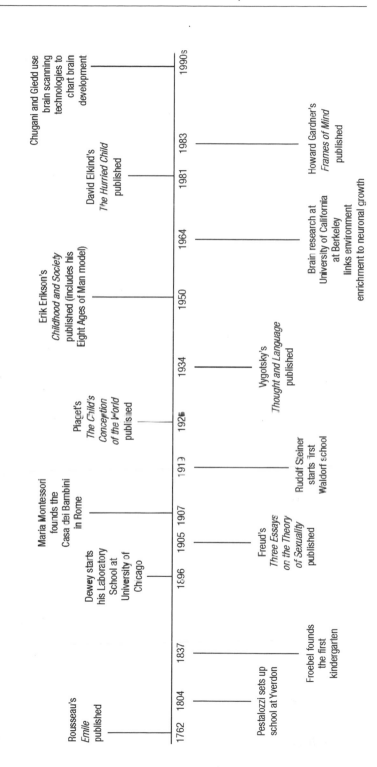

away from the highway and securing it from the impact of human opinion! Cultivate and water the young plant before it dies. Its fruits will one day be your delights. Form an enclosure around your child's soul at an early date" (Rousseau, 1762/1979, p. 38).

Swiss educator Johann Heinrich Pestalozzi borrowed Rousseau's ideas and implemented them within a school framework at Bergdorf and later at Yverdon, Switzerland. He believed that children should learn through active engagement with things in the world and by following their own interests. In his seminal work on education, *How Gertrude Teaches Her Children* (written in 1801), he shared his own personal discovery of the powers of development within the child. As Pestalozzi (1894) wrote:

> The result of attending to this perfecting of the early stages [of a lesson] far outran my expectations. It quickly developed in the children a consciousness of hitherto unknown power, and particularly a general sense of beauty and order. They felt their own power, and the tediousness of the ordinary school-tone vanished like a ghost from my rooms. They wished, –tried, –persevered, –succeeded, and they laughed. Their tone was not that of learners, it was the tone of unknown powers awakened from sleep; of a heart and mind exalted with the feeling of what these powers could and would lead them to do. Children taught children. They tried to put into practice what I told them to do and often came themselves on the track of the means of its execution, from many sides. This self-activity, which had developed itself in many ways in the beginning of learning, worked with great force on the birth and growth of the conviction in me, that all true, all educative instruction must be drawn out of the children themselves, and be born within them. (p. 17)

Pestalozzi in turn influenced German educator Fredrich Froebel, who created the first kindergarten ("children's garden") in the world, with its emphasis on play, concrete learning materials (called "gifts"), and "occupations" that included art activities, gardening, and dance. In his book *The Education of Man,* Froebel (1887) continued his predecessors' use of nature metaphors to describe the development of the young child. Criticizing the manipulative methods of education then used in his country, he wrote:

We grant space and time to young plants and animals because we
know that, in accordance with the laws that live in them, they will
develop properly and grow well; young animals and plants are given
rest, and arbitrary interference with their growth is avoided, because
it is known that the opposite practice would disturb their pure unfolding and sound development; but the young human being is looked
upon as a piece of wax, a lump of clay which man can mold into what
he pleases. (p. 8)

Froebel's kindergartens were shut down by the Prussian government during the political repressions of 1848, but his ideas were
brought to America by German immigrants in the second half of the
19th century.

Human Development Discourse in education received a big
boost in the United States with the work of philosopher and educator John Dewey. In 1896, Dewey and his wife, Alice, founded
the Laboratory School at the University of Chicago, which was to
serve as a fertile ground for trying out innovative educational ideas
based on the child's engagement with real-life experiences in the
context of a democratic community. At the Laboratory School, for
example, students would learn chemistry, physics, and biology by
investigating the processes that went on while they were cooking
their breakfast each morning in class. In his seminal paper "My
Pedagogic Creed," Dewey (1897) made clear his confidence in the
developmental processes of his students:

The child's own instincts and powers furnish the material and give
the starting point for all education. Save as the efforts of the educator
connect with some activity which the child is carrying on of his own
initiative independent of the educator, education becomes reduced to
a pressure from without. It may, indeed, give certain external results
but cannot truly be called educative. Without insight into the psychological structure and activities of the individual, the educative
process will, therefore, be haphazard and arbitrary. If it chances to
coincide with the child's activity it will get a leverage; if it does not, it
will result in friction, or disintegration, or arrest of the child nature.
(p. 77)

Another important influence in the growth of Human Development Discourse that took place around the turn of the 20th century came from the work of Sigmund Freud. His explorations of the unconscious, his emphasis on the importance of early childhood emotional experiences on later life, and his formulation of a stage theory of childhood and adolescent development based upon sexual and aggressive drives (the oral, anal, phallic, latency, and genital stages of development) brought a new dimension to an understanding of how children and adolescents grow and learn (Freud, 1905/2000). Freud's ideas were applied to education by many educators during the 20th century—including A. S. Neill, Carl Rogers, Bruno Bettelheim, and William Glasser—each of whom stressed the destructive nature of repressive learning methods, the importance of emotional expression, and the need for greater sensitivity to the inner worlds of children and adolescence (Bettelheim, 1989; Glasser, 1975; Neill, 1995; Rogers, 1994). In addition, several of Freud's disciples, including Alfred Adler, Carl Jung, and Erik Erikson, would create theories of development that would be used by educators during the 20th century (Erikson, 1993; Hoffman, 1994; Jung, 1969). In Erikson's first published paper—"Psychoanalysis and the Future of Education"—he expressed the hope that "the truth of the healing power of self-knowledge . . . will provide a 'clear vision' resulting in 'a new education' of children" (1935). Erikson in turn influenced psychiatrist Robert Coles, whose narratives of children speaking out about religion, politics, morality, and other important cultural issues, often in the midst of poverty and crisis, have provided a uniquely personal record of the developmental challenges that many children face growing up in a complex world (see, for example, Coles, 1991, 2000, 2003).

Before he became a psychoanalyst, Erik Erikson had trained as a Montessori teacher. Maria Montessori is another 20th-century educator who had a major role in forming the Human Development Discourse in education. The first woman in Italy to receive a medical degree, Montessori developed a great interest in children and in 1907 started a school in a slum area outside of Rome, the Casa dei Bambini ("The House of Children"), which served as a proving ground for many of the ideas, strategies, and materials that would form a part of the Montessori Method, an approach to education that would sweep the world over the next several decades. Her method was, at heart, based on a deep respect for the child's ability to learn about the world without interference from adults. She wrote:

> Supposing I said there was a planet without schools or teachers, study was unknown, and yet the inhabitants—doing nothing but living and walking about—came to know all things, to carry in their minds the whole of learning: would you not think I was romancing? Well, just this, which seems so fanciful as to be nothing but the invention of a fertile imagination, is a reality. It is the child's way of learning. This is the path he follows. He learns everything without knowing he is learning it, and in doing so passes little from the unconscious to the conscious, treading always in the paths of joy and love. (Montessori, 1984, p. 36)

Another thinker known for developing a holistic system of education is German philosopher and mystic Rudolf Steiner, who in 1919 was asked by the owner of the Waldorf Astoria cigarette factory in Stuttgart, Germany, to establish and direct a school for the children of the workers there. His efforts eventually led to the establishment of Waldorf Education, which currently involves more than 800 schools in 40 countries. Steiner believed that children were threefold beings (spirit, soul, and body) who unfolded in three developmental stages of seven years each. The first seven years, according to Steiner, should be dedicated to the development of the child's physical capacities (the education of the hand). The second seven years should involve the cultivation of the child's emotional life (the education of the heart). The third seven years should educate the adolescent's intellectual life (the education of the head). Steiner's unique way of constructing the curriculum gave attention to each of these developmental needs, with the school day divided into three parts. The beginning of the school day involved the head (intellectual work), the middle of the day was dedicated to the heart (stories, music, and rhythm), and the end of the school day was devoted to the hand (physical and hands-on activities) (see Steiner, 1995, 2000).

An additional historical thread in Human Development Discourse began when Swiss epistemologist Jean Piaget's work with Alfred Binet and intelligence testing caused him to be fascinated with the ways in which children think about the world. In a series of remarkable books and articles written from the 1920s to the 1970s, Piaget explored how children think about time, space, number, logic, and many other aspects of the objective world (see, for example, Piaget, 1975, 1998, 2000). He was one of the first researchers to demonstrate (through case studies and naturalistic observations) that children think in qualitatively different ways than adults. He developed a stage theory to describe how children's thinking became more and more complex over time, starting with a sensorimotor period during the first two years of life, a pre-operational (transitional) stage from 3 to 6, an operational stage (the first applications of adultlike logic) from 7 to 11, and a formal operational stage (where the adolescent is capable of thinking without reference to concrete things) from 11 or 12 on. His theories provided a basis for other researchers, including Lawrence Kohlberg, Jerome Bruner, and Howard Gardner, to explore additional aspects of the developmental processes of cognition such as moral judgment, the construction of meaning, and artistic development (see, for example, Bruner, 2004; Gardner, 1991; Kohlberg, 1981). Another student of Piaget, David Elkind, explored the impact developmentally inappropriate educational and cultural practices can have on human growth and learning (1987, 1997, 2001a).

Russian psychologist Lev Vygotsky also had a big impact on understanding children's cognitive development. He examined the development of language in young children and stressed the importance of social context and cultural influences in facilitating human development and learning. He wrote:

> In the process of development the child not only masters the items
> of cultural experience but the habits and forms of cultural behaviour,
> the cultural methods of reasoning. We must, therefore, distinguish the
> main lines in the development of the child's behaviour. First, there is
> the line of natural development of behaviour, which is closely bound
> up with the processes of general organic growth and the maturation
> of the child. Second, there is the line of cultural improvement of the
> psychological functions, the working out of new methods of reason-
> ing, the mastering of the cultural methods of behaviour. (Vygotsky,
> 1929, p. 415)

During the last 35 years, advances in our understanding of the
human brain have added another dimension to Human Development Discourse in education. Starting with studies done in the late
1960s at the University of California at Berkeley (when researchers
discovered the impact that environmental stimulation can have
on brain development in rats), there has been increasing attention
given to how an understanding of brain development in children
and adolescents can help educators facilitate developmentally
appropriate practices in the schools at all levels (see, for example,
Diamond & Hopson, 1998). Researchers have used brain scanning
techniques to examine structural features and metabolic activity
in children's brains from infancy to adolescence (Chugani, 1998;
Giedd, 2004; Giedd et al.,1996, 1999). Many of these studies point
to high levels of activity in the neocortex from early childhood to
around the age of 10, after which these levels generally decline
along with the brain's "plasticity" (its ability to change its architecture at the neuronal level in response to environmental stimulation). Brain researcher Harry Chugani wrote:

> The notion of an extended period during childhood when activity-
> dependent synaptic stabilization occurs has received considerable
> attention recently by those individuals and organizations dealing with
> early intervention to provide "environmental enrichment" and with
> the optimal design of educational curricula. Thus, it now is believed
> by many (including this author) that a biological "window of opportu-
> nity" when learning is efficient and easily retained is perhaps not fully
> exploited by our educational system. (1998, p. 1228)

These rapidly advancing understandings of how the brain develops, while positivistic in nature (the physical and biological aspects of human development must necessarily be so), complement many aspects of Human Development Discourse and will be discussed throughout the rest of this book.

Positive Consequences of Human Development Discourse

In the last chapter, we examined several negative consequences of Academic Achievement Discourse in education. After having examined the definitions, assumptions, and history of Human Development Discourse in this chapter, we now turn to an examination of the *positive* consequences of engaging in Human Development Discourse. It deserves mention here that one of the best reasons to turn the focus of attention toward Human Development Discourse is that it can *reduce* the attention given to Academic Achievement Discourse and as a result can help to lessen the negative consequences of Academic Achievement Discourse. This shift in attention would mean less cheating, less teaching to the test, less manipulation of test results, less use of "study drugs," less emotional stress on students, less grade retention and dropping out, and less disempowerment of students and educators alike. Reductions in these factors would be a major positive consequence. Note that positive consequences discussed below will not occur unless Human Development Discourse is engaged in at a fundamentally deep level. Mere token talk—using Human Development Discourse on opening day at school, at professional development workshops, and in state and federal preambles to laws—will not suffice. This discourse must be a day-to-day activity that informs significant decisions about the lives of students.

Positive Consequence #1: Human Development Discourse engages students in learning activities and coursework that will better prepare them to function in the real world.

Advocates of Academic Achievement Discourse exhort their students to study hard, get good grades, and do well on tests so as to prepare for the future. But what kind of future is this? A future of *more* hard study, grade grubbing, and test taking. The real world is not like that. The real world involves getting along with others, solving commonsense problems, becoming part of a community, and developing competence in a profession that could involve music, art, theater, mechanics, carpentry, or other nonacademic pursuits. A strict focus on academic achievement does not prepare students to join in this rich and complex world. Instead it narrows the focus to only a small part of what goes on in the world. I've often told participants in my workshops that it seems the schools do the best job of preparing kids for one particular job: test manufacturer employees. By the end of high school they have taken thousands of tests, so they must be experts in testing by graduation. The only problem is that there aren't many job openings for test makers! Students are far more ready to take on the world in adulthood if they have been involved in broader programs of study that help them try out different kinds of academic and nonacademic pursuits, understand themselves as learners, develop their creative and problem-solving abilities, and enhance their social skills.

Positive Consequence #2: Human Development Discourse enables all students to shine in their areas of strength.

If all the focus of an educational program is on academics, then students who are school smart will be the only ones who really succeed. At the same time, those who do not possess schoolhouse intelligence but who are accomplished at nonacademic pursuits will have few opportunities to show their abilities. In fact, they will spend most of their time engaged in those activities in which they are *least* competent. I ask readers: How would you function if you had to spend 6 hours a day for 40-plus weeks a year doing the things that you have the hardest time with in life? Would not the temptation to drop out (or misbehave) be strong? On the other hand, a school program based on Human Development Discourse, one that seeks to help kids unfold their potentials by offering courses in music, gardening, architecture, storytelling, painting, and plumbing in addition to reading, math, and science, provides many more opportunities for all kids to succeed as learners.

Positive Consequence #3: Human Development Discourse lessens the need to classify students as learning disabled, attention deficit hyperactivity disorder, academically underachieving, or with other negative labels.

School labels such as learning disabilities and attention deficit disorder came into being in large part because of the rise of Academic Achievement Discourse in the 1960s and 1970s. As noted in the last chapter's history of Academic Achievement Discourse, the 1960s saw the passage of the Elementary and Secondary Education Act, the implementation of the National Assessment of Educational Progress, and the beginning (in 1970) of the use of the word "accountability" in education. The Children with Specific Learning Disabilities Act was passed in 1969, and the term attention deficit disorder was coined by McGill researcher Virginia Douglas in 1972. This was no coincidence. As demands for achievement in reading, writing, and math increased, there arose a need to describe individuals who could not keep up, and the number of children placed in special education classes for academic failure rose accordingly: the number of children in special education has nearly doubled since 1977 (Goldstein, 2003). A corollary to this rise is the suggestion that as Academic Achievement Discourse diminishes in intensity, it is likely that fewer students will need to be placed in special remedial classes, because they will have opportunities for learning and growing in areas of strength through educational practices informed by Human Development Discourse.

Positive Consequence #4: Human Development Discourse enables students to develop competencies and qualities that will ultimately help to make the world a better place.

Helping students get high test scores and gain admission to the nation's best colleges and universities does not correlate to producing human beings who will help solve the problems of war, poverty, overpopulation, and disease. David Halberstam's book *The Best and the Brightest* made the point that some of the most highly educated Ivy League graduates led the United States into the quagmire of the Vietnam War, which resulted in the killing of hundreds of thousands of soldiers and civilians (Halberstam, 1993). More chillingly, a country that produced many of the most highly academically educated people in the world—Germany—evolved into a barbaric Nazi culture that orchestrated the annihilation of millions of innocent people (Shirer, 1990). Academic Achievement Discourse does not facilitate the development of humane conduct and humanitarian behavior. It may in fact inhibit this development by narrowing the focus of learning to a preference for numbers and words over people. Human Development Discourse, on the other hand, has as a major concern the development of individuals who *care* about the world around them and who will ultimately develop in adulthood what Erik Erikson called the quality of "generativity": the capacity to give something back to the community and to the culture (Erikson, 1993). Only in a climate in which service to the community is given equal or superior status to reading, math, and science achievement will this kind of development occur.

Positive Consequence #5: Human Development Discourse helps ameliorate many of the social problems that plague our youth in today's fragmented culture.

It's clear to all educators that many of our nation's young people engage in self-destructive behaviors, such as suicide, drug use, smoking, eating disorders, and alcohol consumption. In addition, they take part in behaviors that are destructive to others, including vandalism, sexual harassment, bullying, and gang violence. A school curriculum that focuses the greater part of its attention on academic learning and test scores has fewer resources available for helping students cope with the struggles of daily living that lead to many of these behaviors. On the other hand, schools that engage in Human Development Discourse tend to create programs that support the mental health needs of students so that these behaviors are less likely to emerge. Such programs include comprehensive counseling and referral services, self-awareness programs, sex education classes, democratic classrooms, prevention programs, character education, mentoring programs, and courses that channel destructive energy into creative pathways such as art, drama, music, and dance. By being concerned with the whole development of students, including their social, emotional, and creative needs, Human Development Discourse is primed to support attitudes and behaviors that are life-affirming and that can help resolve conflicts and nip psychological problems in the bud before they have a chance to explode and damage the lives of students and those around them.

Positive Consequence #6: Human Development Discourse helps students become more of who they really are.

Even if Academic Achievement Discourse results in all students realizing their full academic potential (e.g., every student becoming proficient in reading, math, and science by the year 2014), it will still fall far short of the real goal of educating human beings. As we noted earlier in the chapter, the word "academic" is finite, but the word "human" is infinite. Once we achieve the goal of ensuring that every child achieves academically, then what? Academic Achievement Discourse suggests that nothing more is required: educators have fulfilled their duty. Human Development Discourse, on the other hand, regards 100 percent academic proficiency as only a small part of the development of an individual's potential, a process which is ongoing and ultimately unfathomable. Human Development Discourse realizes that each student has a unique potential to develop her capacities beyond their present state, and more importantly, *beyond even the expectations of teachers*. Academic Achievement Discourse tries to predict the limits to which a student can achieve early in her schooling, through screening tests, I.Q. tests, and "readiness" assessments. Such students are often locked into teachers' self-fulfilling prophecies as a result (Rosenthal & Jacobson, 2003). Human Development Discourse still leaves room for the possibility of a child developing unknown potentials as he or she matures. Biographical studies of great people have shown that many of them were not predicted to do very well in life (see for example, Goertzel, Goertzel, & Hansen, 2004). As musician Pablo Casals (1981) wrote:

> What do we teach our children in school? We teach them that two and two make four, and that Paris is the capital of France. When will we also teach them what they are? We should say to each of them: Do you know what you are? You are a marvel. You are unique. In all of the world there is no other child exactly like you. In the millions of years that have passed there has never been another child like you. And look at your body—what a wonder it is! Your legs, your arms, your cunning fingers, the way you move! You may become a Shakespeare, a Michelangelo, a Beethoven. You have the capacity for anything. Yes, you are a marvel. (p. 295)

Positive Consequence #7: Human Development Discourse gives educators and students more control over their learning environment.

In today's Academic Achievement Discourse climate, in which the NCLB law mandates that schools make adequate yearly progress, teachers are forced to adopt programs and use teaching methods that may not be congruent with their own teaching philosophies. Their own abilities and integrity as educators are ignored, and as a result they become disempowered. This disempowerment is passed on to students, who find that their own interests and learning styles are not taken into consideration as school leaders focus on narrow academic goals. As long as academic achievement tests remain the primary arbiter of learning progress, educators and students will be chained to those methods and programs that best facilitate achieving the highest test scores. These are often methods and programs that look suspiciously like the tests themselves. Human Development Discourse, on the other hand, is concerned with the development of teachers and students alike (note the use of the words "professional *development*" in describing teacher workshops and seminars). Autonomy is an important aspect of human development that is particularly honored in Human Development Discourse. In programs inspired by Human Development Discourse, teachers are respected as experts of their craft, and students are able to make significant choices about their learning experiences.

Positive Consequence #8: Human Development Discourse results in fewer discipline problems in schools.

When the focus of education is academic achievement, those students who won't or can't participate in the process are more likely to engage in a variety of misbehaviors in the classroom. As a result, educators are forced to use any number of discipline methods, including behavior modification strategies, assertive discipline programs, school expulsion, and punishment. Over a quarter of a million children are physically hit by teachers in the United States every year (National Association of School Psychologists, 2005). Academic Achievement Discourse mandates that continual progress be made in the acquisition of core academic subjects, and if students attempt to sabotage this process, time and energy must be put into either reforming such students or removing them from the classroom.

Human Development Discourse, on the other hand, views "discipline problems" as part of the developmental process of students, and thus regards these problems as opportunities for change and growth. Instead of simply having to make the misbehaviors *stop*, as in Academic Achievement Discourse, Human Development Discourse is concerned with helping educators and students understand the underlying emotional, social, or cognitive reasons why these behaviors exist (the word "discipline" after all, means "to learn"). A student may throw a paper airplane at the teacher, for example, because he's bored, anxious, depressed, confused, angry, or any number of other reasons. By regarding these behaviors as "obstacles to growth," rather than "bad behaviors," Human Development Discourse is able to generate solutions to help provide students with safety, academic help, social skills training, or any number of other developmental interventions that get at the heart of the difficulty. In addition, when students are engaged in classroom activities that engage their social, emotional, creative, physical, and spiritual selves, they are far less likely to *need* to engage in activities designed to subvert the learning process.

Positive Consequence #9: Human Development Discourse encourages innovation and diversity learning programs.

As noted earlier, Academic Achievement Discourse narrows the focus of the curriculum and disempowers educators who are forced to teach to the test. Programs that use lockstep approaches to learning, such as Direct Instruction, keep teachers from injecting their own creativity and uniqueness into the classroom. Human Development Discourse, on the other hand, values such qualities as creativity, individuality, and innovation, and provides a climate within which teachers and students can engage in open-ended discussions, individualized projects, serendipitous learning (exciting ideas that emerge unexpectedly and deserve to be explored), and innovative approaches that show promise in developing a student's social, cognitive, emotional, moral, or creative abilities. Some of these approaches include multiple intelligences, brain-based learning, community service projects, affective education, and constructivist learning. Such approaches are frequently branded by Academic Achievement Discourse advocates as untested, unreliable, and faddish, and are blamed for lowering test scores nationwide. These characterizations are understandable, because Academic Achievement Discourse criteria for success are based on quantitative research and high test results. Human Development Discourse defines success in terms of promoting the growth of whole human beings and views progress in terms of a student's increasing ability to care, to create, to feel confident, to be inspired, to solve problems, to think deeply, and to live deeply. Consequently, it is constantly on the lookout for interesting strategies, courses, and programs that will help unfold the potentials of children and adolescents in these and other areas.

Positive Consequence #10: Human Development Discourse promotes the establishment of developmentally appropriate practices and discourages the use of developmentally inappropriate practices in schools.

Perhaps the most important positive consequence of Human Development Discourse is that it will lead to a greater use of teaching approaches and programs that are designed to meet the developmental needs of students at specific age levels from early childhood to late adolescence. Academic Achievement Discourse recognizes developmental needs primarily in only one way: in the structure of schooling by age/grade levels (e.g., preschool, kindergarten, primary, upper elementary, middle school/junior high, and high school). In addition, there is some recognition in Academic Achievement Discourse that content and method must be adjusted to the age level of a student.

However, Academic Achievement Discourse has increasingly imposed its narrow agenda on the entire spectrum of ages and developmental levels. This broad application has resulted in developmental abuses such as giving two hours of homework to kindergartners, forcing academic achievement aspirations on stressed-out high school seniors, and ignoring the impact of puberty and social and emotional growth in early adolescence while racing through an impersonal academic curriculum. Such developmentally inappropriate practices may unwittingly contribute to a variety of social ills, including attention and learning problems, stress-related illnesses, and even school violence (Elkind, 1997, 2001a, 2001b). Human Development Discourse is, on the other hand, by its very nature committed to teaching methods and school programs that meet the specific developmental needs of students.

The last four chapters of this book will focus on how Human Development Discourse should be used to inform appropriate teaching practices in the face of an increasingly intense Academic Achievement Discourse that ignores important developmental needs in students. I propose specific developmental aims at four levels of schooling: early childhood, elementary school, middle school/junior high school, and high school. I argue that the main focus of early childhood education should be *play,* that the main focus of elementary school should be *learning how the world works*, that the main focus of middle school/junior high school should be *social, emotional, and metacognitive development,* and finally, that the main focus of high school should be *preparing students to live independently in the real world.*

In the four chapters that follow, I will discuss each of these four levels of schooling and their respective developmental goals. In each chapter, I will describe the unique developmental features of the children or adolescents at that level (recognizing that individual students vary considerably in their developmental rates). I will include information about important biological and neurological changes that occur at each level, sociological and anthropological information about how human cultures have traditionally educated children or adolescents at each level, and psychological knowledge about how children or adolescents perceive, feel, think, and relate to others and to the objective world. In each case, I will show how the unique features of students at each developmental level have important consequences regarding what kind of teaching programs and approaches are most suitable for them. I will also indicate in each chapter how Academic Achievement Discourse has failed to recognize these developmental needs, and in some cases, has worked actively against them. Finally, I will describe the specific kinds of curricula, teaching techniques, learning strategies, and school programs that are developmentally appropriate for each level, and which practices are to be avoided. In each chapter, I will include examples of schools that engage in the developmentally appropriate practices I have described. These stand as representative examples of *the best schools* in the country. As we will see, the best schools are not necessarily the ones with the highest test scores, but those that seek to develop the best aspects of each human being as he or she grows toward maturity.

For Further Study

1. How often do you and your colleagues engage in Human Development Discourse? Look at the following words and phrases:

Blocks to growth
Character
Child-centered
Cognitive growth
Creative unfoldment
Creativity
Curiosity
Developmental challenges
Developmental goals
Developmental lines
Developmentally appropriate
    (or inappropriate) practices
Developmental pathways
Developmental trajectories
Early childhood trauma
Emotional growth

Flourishing
Flow
Fostering growth
Human growth and
    development
Human potential
Identity formation
Immaturity
Individuality
Individualized learning
Individuation
Integrity
Ipsative measurements
Learning needs
Maturation
Maturity

Moral development	Sensitive periods
Natural learning	Social growth
Nurturing	Spiritual growth
Optimal development	Stages of life
Physical growth	Transformation
Resilience	Uniqueness
Self-actualization	Windows of opportunity
Self-expression	

Notice during a typical school day how often words on the list are used in conversations or written communications with students, teachers, administrators, or parents. Are there particular contexts in which this discourse is used more often (e.g., professional development workshops, assemblies, coaching sessions)? Keep a one-day written record of every time a word or phrase on this list appears in your conversations or in communications that you've written or read. Discuss the results with colleagues. Add any words or phrases not found on the list that you believe also constitute a part of Human Development Discourse.

2. Discuss with your colleagues which particular positive consequences of Human Development Discourse described in this chapter apply to your own school setting. Give concrete examples from your school day. What other positive consequences not specifically mentioned in this chapter also occur in your school setting as a result of Human Development Discourse?

3. Choose a book written by a key Human Development Discourse thinker (e.g., Montessori, Steiner, Dewey, Piaget, Elkind), read it with a group of colleagues, and then meet to discuss the book. (Note: Check the References section of this book for examples of books written by thinkers cited in this chapter.) What sorts of assumptions about human growth and learning are made by the educator you have chosen? Are these assumptions in sync with those of your own school or learning environment? Why or why not? What is there in this thinker's philosophy or practice that might be applied to your own educational setting?

4. Investigate qualitative research methodologies, either alone or with a group of colleagues. (Note: Check the References section for examples of books on qualitative methodologies cited on page 45). What do you see as the advantages of using qualitative research in assessing school learning? What are the disadvantages? Plan and carry out a research project in your educational setting (e.g., classroom, counseling, administration) that uses one or more of the qualitative methods you've learned about. Compare the results with those typically obtained using quantitative measurements to assess school learning (e.g., test results). Discuss the differences that you observe in the kinds of information obtained in each case. What kinds of questions about the value of different kinds of knowledge does this project risk?

3

Early Childhood Education Programs: Play

In a Michigan kindergarten, Joshua Mullins grows germs in a petri dish, practices Spanish vocabulary, and completes homework by writing in his journal (MacDonald, 2005). In San Diego, California, teachers' efforts to lower reading benchmarks for kindergarten children alarm a district official who declares: "When the bar becomes lower, very often teachers can have a lower expectation for children" (Gao, 2005, para. 12). In a Florida school district, kindergarten lessons cover reading, writing, math, science, history, geography, civics, and economics (Feller, 2005). In a Wisconsin school district, benchmarks for kindergarten include "understanding the concept of one-to-one correspondence," "making a simple graph and sharing observations," and "demonstrating knowledge of penmanship guidelines." Academic preschools are shooting up across the United States. These schools have 4-year-olds practicing phonics skills, filling out activity worksheets, and writing books (see, for example, Whitehurst, 2001).

Thirty years ago, such activities at the preschool or kindergarten level would have been inconceivable to all but the most achievement-driven educators. Today, they are common practice. The "children's gardens" created by Friedrich Froebel 150 years ago are turning into learning factories for the very young. Early childhood education once was a domain in which Human Development Discourse was the primary conversation taking place among educators. Today, it is Academic Achievement Discourse that reigns. In this chapter, I'll focus on early childhood education and describe what the real developmental needs of young children are, how play is the single best way in which those needs can be met in preschools and kindergartens, and how to distinguish between early childhood programs that use developmentally inappropriate practices and those that use developmentally appropriate practices.

Developmental Needs of Young Children (Ages 3–6)

Academic Achievement Discourse seeks to create a continuity of curricula from early childhood education into elementary school and beyond. Programs that use Academic Achievement Discourse phrases such as "bridging the preK–elementary divide" and "creating seamless transitions from kindergarten to elementary school," hide the fact that in most cases, they seek to make early childhood education more like elementary school and not the reverse (see Wiltz, 2005). And yet, young children live—socially, cognitively, and emotionally—in a qualitatively different world than older children. The work of Jean Piaget, in particular, has made educators aware of how vastly different the developmental needs of young children are from older children. Piaget used the term "pre-operational" to describe the thinking of children from the age of 2 or 3 to 6. By this he meant that young children don't yet use logical operations (numeration, seriation, reversibility thinking, etc.) in their mental processes in understanding the world around them. In his book *The Child's Conception of the World*, Piaget (1975) described some of the ways in which young children think about the world. They use animism—that is, they see inanimate objects as alive. Piaget observed a 3-year-old who had scratched herself on a wall point to her hand and say: "Who made that mark? . . . It hurts where the wall hit me" (p. 212). The world of a preschooler is dynamic and even mythological in character. Piaget noted that a 4-year-old boy said, "There's the moon, it's round." Then, when a cloud covered the moon, the child commented, "Look now, it's been killed" (p. 210).

Human developmental pioneer Heinz Werner (1980) used the term "physiognomic perception" to describe how young children look at the world. He wrote:

> All of us, at some time or other, have had this experience [in adulthood]. A landscape, for instance, may be seen suddenly in immediacy as expressing a certain mood—it may be gay or melancholy or pensive. This mode of perception differs radically from the more everyday perception in which things are known according to their "geometrical-technical" matter-of-fact qualities, as it were. In our own sphere there is one field where objects are commonly perceived as directly expressing an inner life. This is in our perception of the faces and bodily movements of human beings and higher animals. Because the human physiognomy can be adequately perceived only in terms of its immediate expression, I have proposed the term physiognomic perception for this mode of cognition in general. (p. 69)

As an example, Werner cited the case of a 4-year-old girl who saw some cards on which angular figures were drawn and exclaimed, "Ugh! What a lot of prickles and thorns!" She hesitated to pick up the cards, thinking that the thorns would prick her fingers. In another case, a 5½-year-old girl was walking in the rain with her mother during dusk and said: "I can't see a thing, it's so foggy. Everything is like whispering!" (Werner, 1980, pp. 72–74). Russian children's author Kornei Chukovsky (1963) regarded children from 2 to 5 as "linguistic geniuses" because of their ability to use thought and language in fresh ways, such as in the case of the child who said, "Don't turn out the light—I won't be able to see how to sleep" (p. 3). The experience of synesthesia, in which sights are heard, colors tasted, and sounds touched, is much more common in early development (see, for example, Baron-Cohen, 1996). The young child's imagination is more vivid than the older child's, and in some cases it reaches the level of *eidetic* imagery, where inner images are seen as clearly as outer perceptions (see, Giray, Altkin, Vaught, & Roodin, 1976).

The young child's metaphorical, imaginative, synesthetic, and magical ways of approaching the world are, in many ways, a reflection of what is going on at the neurological level. The brain of a young child is structurally and functionally different from the brain of an older child. As brain researcher Marian Diamond (Diamond & Hopson, 1998) pointed out:

> The energy use in a 2-year-old [brain] is equal to an adult's. And then, *the levels keep right on rising* until, by age 3, the child's brain is *twice* as active as an adult's. This metaphoric crackling, bristling, sparkling, and glowing of brain cells remains at double the adult rate until about age 9 or 10; at that time, metabolism begins dropping and reaches adult levels by age 18. (p. 54)

At the same time, the young child has an abundance of dendrites (connections between neurons) undergoing a process of pruning, in which neuronal connections are reinforced or discarded depending upon what types of stimulation the child receives or doesn't receive from the environment (Chugani, 1998). Social and emotional factors in the child's surroundings are particularly important in this process of brain development (Siegel, 2001).

In addition, the young child's nervous system has not yet been fully myelinated in many areas of the brain. Myelination is the process by which axons are sheathed or insulated to permit the efficient passage of electric impulses through the brain (see Klingberg, Vaidya, Gabrieli, Moseley, & Hedehus, 1999). This incomplete myelination of the brain may help to explain why many of the young child's perceptions and thoughts are so different from the thinking of older kids and adults. The incredible plasticity of the child's brain points to the importance of the child's surroundings—

a safe and caring social and emotional space coupled with a hands-on interactive environment—in promoting healthy neurological growth. The high metabolic activity in a young child's brain suggests that the child should be exposed to dynamic, creative, and multisensory experiences.

The Developmental Importance of Play

Children's play represents the single best way in which the above developmental requirements can be met. Play *is* a dynamic, ever-changing process that is multisensory, interactive, creative, and imaginative. When children play, they have their *whole* brain stimulated, not just specific areas related to formal academic skills. Russian psychologist Lev Vygotsky (1929) wrote: "It seems to me that from the point of view of development, play is not the predominant form of activity, but is, in a certain sense, the leading source of development in preschool years" (p. 415). Play facilitates a child's physical and sensorimotor development as she runs, jumps, digs, acts, paints, draws, and in other ways has direct contact with the living earth and the culture around her. It promotes social learning as she plays with other kids, creating roles based on what she sees in the social world around her, adjusting her own play behavior to the needs and demands of her peers. It supports emotional growth as the child is able to project her own fears, joys, jealousies, angers, and ambitions onto toys, puppets, and other playthings, and work out her feelings about a wide range of concerns in constructive ways. It supports cognitive development as the child works symbolically with art materials, dramatic improvisation, and other modes of representation, constructing patterns of meaning from interactions with things and people (see Singer & Singer, 1990).

But great as the above benefits seem, they are nothing compared with what is most extraordinary about play: play serves as a mediator between what is *possible* and what is *actual*. As developmental psychiatrist David Winnicott (1982) put it:

> This area of playing is not inner psychic reality. It is outside the
> individual, but it is not the external world. Into this play area the child
> gathers objects or phenomena from external reality and uses these
> in the service of some sample derived from inner or personal reality.
> Without hallucinating the child puts out a sample of dream potential
> and lives with this sample in a chosen setting of fragments from exter-
> nal reality. (p. 14)

When children play in this way, they mix the contents of their imaginations (things that are merely *possible*) with the contents of the real world (blocks, toys, costumes, lofts), and through their own creative acts they bring into the world something sponta- neous, novel, and unique. An empty refrigerator box becomes a spaceship. A piece of cloth becomes the shawl of an Arabian princess. A group of blocks becomes a horde of prehistoric animals in a jungle. This process of play may be the single most important thing that humans do. Some scientists have suggested that it was by playing that human beings developed their frontal lobes (Fur- low, 2001). The Dutch historian Johan Huizinga (1986) in his classic work on play, *Homo Ludens* (Man at Play), suggested that play "as a social impulse [is] older than culture itself. . . . Ritual grew up in sacred play; poetry was born in play and nourished on play; music and dancing were pure play. . . . We have to conclude that civiliza- tion is, in its earliest phases, played" (p. 173).

We can see the importance of play to the development of civili- zation by listening to the great thinkers of the world describe their own accomplishments in terms of play. Isaac Newton once wrote: "I do not know what I may appear to the world; but to myself I seem to have been only like a boy playing on the sea shore and divert- ing himself and then finding a smoother pebble or a prettier shell than ordinary while the greater ocean of truth lay all undiscovered before me" (cited in Brewster, 2005, p. 407). Nuclear physicist and father of the atomic bomb, J. Robert Oppenheimer once said, "There are children playing on the streets who could solve some of my top physics problems, because they have modes of perception I lost long ago" (cited in McLuhan & Fiore, 1967, p. 93). Frank Lloyd

Wright traced his own beginnings as an architect back to his first experiences with simple wooden blocks in a Froebel kindergarten (see Rubin, 1989). Alexander Fleming, the Scottish scientist who discovered penicillin, said: "I play with microbes. It is very pleasant to break rules" (cited in Cole, 1988, p. C16). It may be that virtually every significant contribution to culture originally stemmed from a playful act that had its seeds in childhood. This extraordinary feature of play, coupled with its social, emotional, physical, and cognitive benefits, makes play the central developmental activity around which all other early childhood education activities must revolve.

Developmentally Inappropriate Practices

Sadly, in our culture, play is undergoing a significant deterioration. One of the world's greatest experts on play, New Zealand researcher Brian Sutton-Smith, suggests that the typical image now of a child at play is of a single child sitting in front of a television set or video game, playing with his action figures (see Hansen, 1998). This isn't play. Neither are soccer games or other competitive sports events that take place on a regular basis in every community. Play is an open-ended experience initiated by children that involves pretense, rough-and-tumble activity, or the spontaneous use of real objects for creative activity. Play is becoming more of an endangered species in early childhood programs as academic demands increase. In this section, I'd like to look at some of the developmentally inappropriate practices that have replaced play in kindergartens and preschools around the country.

Teaching of Formal Math and Literacy Skills

Educators who employ Academic Achievement Discourse frequently point to brain research, and in particular to the plasticity of the child's brain, as a justification for teaching young children to read, write, and do math. Yet brain research is actually suggesting quite the reverse, demonstrating that the young child's brain is not yet ready for these abstract formal skills, but rather should be devoted to imaginative, metaphorical, multisensory, and playful learning.

Piaget led the way in pointing out how children advance cognitively by engaging in a naturalistic hands-on exploration of the real world. It is interesting to note that Piaget was often asked by American educators how the stages of cognitive development could be speeded up (a good example of Academic Achievement Discourse at work). Piaget called this "the American question" (Duckworth, 1979, p. 303). The stages of development shouldn't be forced, he suggested, but rather should come from a natural interaction of the child with a rich environment.

One of Piaget's chief proponents in the United States, psychologist David Elkind (2001b), points out how developmentally inappropriate it is to teach math too early:

> It is only at age 6 or 7, when they have attained what Piaget calls "concrete operations," that children can construct the concept of a "unit," the basis for understanding the idea of interval numbers. To attain the unit concept, children must come to understand that every number is both like every other number, in the sense that it is a number, and at the same time different in its order of enumeration. Once children attain the unit concept, their notion of number is abstract and divorced from particular things, unlike nominal and ordinal numbers. Mathematical operations like addition, subtraction, and multiplication can be performed only on numbers that represent units that can be manipulated without reference to particular things. (p. 13)

Similarly, with respect to the inappropriate teaching of reading to young children, Elkind wrote:

> To read phonemically, a child must be able to recognize that a letter can be pronounced differently depending on the context. A child who can read "hat," "cat," and "sat" may have trouble with "ate," "gate," and "late." Likewise, a child who knows "pin" may have trouble with "spin" because it involves a blend of consonants that may throw kids off. In Piaget's terminology, "concrete" operations are required for this highest level of reading. (p. 14)

This absence of developmental readiness for formal lessons in reading and math in early childhood may help to explain the downward trend of some students who are taught their letters, numbers, and other rote skills in early intervention programs such as Head Start. Research suggests that children who have had this type of early intervention tend to perform better in the early grades where rote skills are most helpful, but by the later grades, when the cognitive demands of literacy really kick in, they have washed out their gains (Currie & Thomas, 1995).

Standardized Testing

Beginning in 2003, the federal government began using tests in the Head Start program (Rothstein, 2004). Over half a million 4-year-olds sit for a 20- to 30-minute standardized test that covers their achievement in literacy and number skills. These tests are in addition to others used to assess program quality, conduct research, and evaluate the progress of children on a regular basis. At the kindergarten level, most states use standardized readiness tests and screening tests that are given before entering kindergarten and before graduating from kindergarten.

All of this testing is going on despite warnings from national organizations for young children suggesting that such practices should stop. In 1987, the National Association for the Education of Young Children (NAEYC) issued a position paper that cautioned against most forms of testing before the age of 8. Instead of standardized tests, NAEYC recommended the use of developmentally appropriate practices such as informal assessments, including teacher observations and portfolios. The National Association of School Psychologists (2005) noted in its position paper on early childhood assessment that "evidence from research and practice in early childhood assessment indicates that issues of technical adequacy are more difficult to address with young children who have little test-taking experience, short attention spans, and whose development is rapid and variable" (para. 2). The Association for

Childhood Education International issued a position statement that "sets forth unequivocally the belief that *all* testing of young children in preschool and grades K–2 . . . should cease" (Perrone, 1991, p. 141). It noted that standardized testing in the early years causes stress, does not provide useful information, leads to harmful tracking and labeling of children, causes teaching to the test, and fails to set conditions for cooperative learning and problem solving.

Computers and Other Forms of High-Tech Learning

In the late 1980s, only 25 percent of licensed preschools in the United States had computers. Now, virtually every preschool has one. Due in large part to the research of MIT scientist Seymour Papert and others in the field of computer science, computer activities at the kindergarten level have been regarded as a cutting-edge learning tool. Kinder-LOGO, for example, is a software program based on Papert's work that lets students explore letters, numbers, colors, and shapes, and that is advertised as teaching spatial awareness, attributes, patterns, cause-and-effect relationships, and problem solving. Similarly, television has been considered a staple of early childhood education ever since *Sesame Street* began broadcasting its letter and number shapes back in 1969. Yet when we remind ourselves of how young children think about the world, we realize that learning through technology may not be as developmentally appropriate as many educators apparently think it is.

Television and computer screens are not the sensory-rich environments that young children need in order to exercise their multimodal brains. History and education professor Douglas Sloan (1985) asked, "What is the effect of the flat, two-dimensional, visual, and externally supplied image, and of the lifeless though florid colors of the viewing screen, on the development of the young child's own inner capacity to bring to birth living, mobile images of his own?" (p. 8). Young children need hands-on interaction with the content of the real world. Instead, television and computer software offer virtually no real interaction with the world except for the manipulation of a mouse, joystick, or remote control device (Cuffaro, 1984).

Young children require safe and meaningful social and emotional experiences with peers and adults. Although computer advocates often point out that children can interact with classmates and the teacher while working with a software program, this argument does not justify the computer itself, just the interactions that occur around it. Perhaps the biggest problem with computers is that children can't *play* with them (in the deeper sense of the term) because the environment has been so highly structured and delimited by the software designer. Educator Jane Healy (1999), who has written extensively on the misuse of computers and television in early childhood education, notes that as a result of this, "teachers of young children lament the fact that many now have to be taught to play symbolically or pretend—previously a symptom only of mentally or emotionally disordered youngsters" (p. 64). In my own investigations, I've suggested that one consequence of the rise of technologies and the demise of play, especially in the early years, may be an increase in the number of children identified as having ADD/ADHD (Armstrong, 2003b, 2005). Most educators have abandoned their critique of high-tech tools in early childhood education programs because of the downward pressure of Academic Achievement Discourse on early childhood educators to use computers to help prepare kids for academic skills, and because of the intense corporate push to find new markets for high technology products (see Alliance for Childhood, 2000).

Homework, a Longer School Day, Less Nap Time, and Less Recess

When my wife, who is a child psychotherapist, told me a few years ago that she was working with a kindergarten-age child who had been given two hours of homework to do that evening, I could hardly believe what I was hearing. "Child abuse" is what immediately came to mind. Now I've come to learn that homework is regularly handed out in kindergartens all over the country. One Minnesota school district, for example, has homework expectations for kindergarten students that include practicing the letters and their sounds, practicing sight words and word families that are part of the district's reading series, completing "Dear Family" homework sheets, and "practive" (Note: The district did not do its homework and spelled the word wrong on its Internet site!) putting sounds together to make words via blending (e.g., c-a-t). Academic Achievement Discourse has made this kind of practice perfectly acceptable to use with 5-year-olds in thousands of kindergartens across the country.

Fortunately, there are school districts out there that disagree, including a Virginia district that declares on its Web site: "In general we do not believe that homework is appropriate for kindergarten age students. This age learns through play and that is what we feel they should be doing at home" (Burbank Elementary School, n.d.).

Along with homework comes increasing demands for a longer school day. As one *New York Times* reporter observed: "More school districts are offering a full 7-hour day of kindergarten because they found that traditional three-hour programs did not allow time for the math, language arts, and science lessons that are becoming standard fare" (Zernike, 2000, p. A1). Naturally, something has to give, and it is usually nap time, recess, free play, and, tragically, the child himself. "After a full day," the reporter wrote, "some parents report that their children arrive home at 3:45 and promptly put on their pajamas. One student falls asleep in the car on the way home, although he lives only two blocks from school" (Zernike, 2000, p. A1). Depriving young children of play experiences, the reverie of imagination, and open-ended explorations with the world around them contributes to the acceleration, fragmentation, and deterioration of young children's developmental possibilities.

The Best Early Childhood Programs: Developmentally Appropriate Practices

Although early childhood education programs appear to be only increasing the academic load on young children, there are exemplary programs out there that model what developmentally appropriate learning should look like in the preschool and kindergarten years.

Developmental Preschools and Kindergartens

A good example is Roseville Community Preschool (RCP) in Roseville, California. Founded by parent and educator Bev Bos 32 years ago, RCP is a nonprofit, parent-participation community school that embraces play as its bottom line. The school rules are: "run, jump, dig, explore, talk, build, tear down, pour, yell, saw, hammer, paint, ride, imagine, sing, wonder, measure, ponder, play, be alone, examine, experiment, express, daydream" (Bos & Chapman, 2005, p. xv). Outside, there are spaces to run, sand piles, a block table, gardens, platforms in trees, and a room for mechanical things, including a ship structure with ladders and platforms, a mast, a wheel, a sail, and ropes and pulleys. Inside there is a fish tank, a loft, a cargo-net bridge, trucks, tubes, and tubs and gutters (for sand and water play). Centers for experimentation abound, such as a place of stones, sand, pipettes, food color, and water to combine and explore, pour, mold, and change. There is a dress-up room, an art area, and a child-sized room containing miniature beds, a stove, a refrigerator, a table, chairs, dolls, books, and cooking utensils.

As Bos puts it, "There is no teacher's voice controlling and directing here, just the occasional word of encouragement and the sharing of an idea, a dialogue, a conversation, a scribed story, or a song" (Bos & Chapman, 2005, p. 7). Wander around the school and you will see children painting, digging in sand, make-believe fishing in a puddle of water, building with blocks, putting on plays, planting seeds, hanging from trees, swinging on swings, playing

hide-and-seek, exploring the natural surroundings, cooking with
Play-Doh, experimenting with simple science materials, singing,
and living. One visitor to the school reported: "I was fascinated to
find a preschool with indoor and outdoor space that was, and still
is, very different from preschools elsewhere. Why is this school
different? It is different because children have freedom to become
totally engrossed in play with water, ice, sand, paint, wood, and
words. Time for wonder and exploring are foremost in the ways the
teachers support the children. I always come away from this place
with a feeling that it is unique and could be an example of the kind
of surroundings in which children could thrive, grow and carry
with them the strengths of who they are. The strong sense of self
that they develop, I believe, will be part of their core for life" (Bos &
Chapman, 2005, p. 5).

Reggio Emilia Schools

Another excellent example of how early childhood education can
be practiced is seen in the Reggio Emilia schools. Situated in northern Italy, the town of Reggio Emilia first began to reform its school
system in the ruins of World War II. It opened its first preschools
in 1963. A central feature of the preschools is a focus on a child-
centered approach to curriculum development. In Reggio Emilia
schools, teachers look for cues from the children as to how a curriculum (they call it an "emergent curriculum") will unfold.

For example, at one school, teachers noticed that many of the
5- and 6-year-old children were bringing dinosaur toys to school,
and that the children's play sometimes spontaneously turned to
dinosaurs. Teachers gathered together to discuss the possibilities
among themselves, and then began to initiate with a small group
of interested children an investigation into the world of dinosaurs.
The children drew dinosaurs, talked about them, shared ideas from
their drawings, and thought about questions relating to dinosaurs
that had emerged from their earlier play experiences. Later on,
they were asked where they could find out more information about

dinosaurs, and based on their answers, they visited a local library and brought the books they had borrowed back to the *atelier* (a word meaning "artist's studio"), which served as the central locus for their project.

These books gave rise to more questions and led to the children inviting friends and relatives to visit the school and share what they knew about the subject (a special letter was composed and written by the dinosaur group). Over the next few weeks many people came by, including a father, a grandmother, and an expert from a local nature society, to share their knowledge. Children prepared questions for them in advance.

At the same time, children were making dinosaurs out of clay, painting them, and drawing them with chalk. One group of four boys who were making a large dinosaur out of clay began discussing how they could make a really huge dinosaur. This led to a discussion among teachers and children about how to build a really big dinosaur. Out of this conversation, the importance of determining what kind of dinosaur emerged. After more discussion, the children took a vote and *Tyrannosaurus rex* won by close election over *Stegosaurus*. After spontaneously dividing into smaller groups, the children created three-dimensional models of the dinosaur. Then, emerging out of their curiosity with the actual size of a dinosaur, the children drew a two-dimensional representation of *Diplodocus* that was 27 meters long on their school field. This process of free play, coupled with respect for and close attention by teachers to the thoughts, desires, and productions of children at play, served to create a learning environment of trust, excitement, and discovery. Reggio Emilia schools make children's spontaneous play the central event around which any learning revolves (see Edwards, Gandini, & Foreman, 1998).

Imaginative and Creative Learning

A third example of developmentally appropriate early childhood education comes from Waldorf education (Steiner, 1995, 2000).

Created more than 80 years ago by Austrian philosopher and educator Rudolf Steiner, Waldorf schools emphasize artistic development, cross-cultural enrichment, and a deep regard for the imaginative and creative worlds of children. When a person walks into a Waldorf kindergarten it is like entering a fairy-tale wonderland (Armstrong, 1988). The classroom setting has a storybook look about it, with walls swirled in peach-toned and sky-blue pastels; a ceiling that is naturalistically curved rather than straight and perpendicular; furniture, carpets, and play equipment made from all natural materials; and plants and other living things in abundance.

Although many Waldorf schools are privately run, there are an increasing number of public charter schools using Waldorf methods. At John Morse Waldorf Methods School, which is part of the Sacramento City Unified School District in California, kindergarten children play at creating fantasy worlds from tree stumps, brightly colored scarves, and homemade dolls shaped to look like little elves, fierce dragons, and brave knights. The teacher assembles the children by sweetly singing their names ("*Na*-than"), and leads them in simple movement activities allowing them to become, for the moment, giants, pixies, and gnomes. As in Roseville Community Preschool and the Reggio Emilia schools, simple children's play is regarded as the most important activity going on in the classroom. Waldorf kindergartens use simple wooden blocks, unfinished wooden toys, natural fabrics for dress-up, and naturally made dolls with a minimum of features, so that the imagination of the child can fill in the details. Formal reading is not taught in kindergarten; in first grade children begin to learn the alphabet.

As one Waldorf educator put it: "There are indications that children who learn to read before age six or seven lose their early advantages, for they lose interest in reading and may eventually suffer burnout. This is not surprising when one thinks of how dull reading and learning are without benefit of imagination to bring them alive. In contrast, in my experience, the children who are the best players in the kindergarten and have the most active fantasy tend to become the most imaginative elementary pupils with the greatest interest in reading. They also tend to be the best adjusted emotionally, both as children and even as adolescents and adults" (Almon, 2004, para. 35).

The programs described above are only three examples of developmentally appropriate early childhood education (ECE) programs. There are many other examples around the world. Although there are no hard-and-fast rules to determine whether an ECE program is developmentally appropriate (such rules would probably be antithetical to Human Development Discourse), there are a general set of criteria that could be used to place a program on a continuum ranging from developmentally appropriate on the one end to developmentally inappropriate on the other. An early childhood education program is developmentally appropriate to the extent that it values spontaneous play, multisensory and hands-on learning, natural environments (e.g., lofts, gardens, plants, the arts, animals), and a child-centered approach to learning. Conversely, an ECE program is developmentally inappropriate to the extent that it doesn't contain the above elements, and instead emphasizes formal lessons in reading, writing, math, and other academic subjects; the use of high-tech tools such as computers and television; the assignment of homework; the employment of standardized testing; a long school day that minimizes nap time and other free-time experiences; and a teacher-centered approach to learning. The words "readiness," "early intervention," "academic kindergarten," and "play with a purpose" are often red flags indicating that an early childhood education program has moved away from the Human Development Discourse end of the continuum and moved toward the Academic Achievement Discourse side (see Figure 3.1 for examples of developmentally appropriate and inappropriate practices in early childhood education).

Naturally, many (if not most) ECE programs combine aspects of both discourses. However, at a time when Academic Achievement Discourse is the overwhelming voice in education, the movement in many early childhood education programs is primarily toward a more formal, technological, and academic approach. That this

Figure 3.1

**Developmentally Inappropriate and Appropriate Practices
in Early Childhood Education**

Developmentally Inappropriate Practices	Developmentally Appropriate Practices
Artificial classroom environment	Open-ended play
Long school day	Short school day
Elimination of naps or recess	Nap time
Instruction in formal academic skills (e.g., reading, writing, mathematics, science)	Informal learning all the time
Homework	Parent involvement at school
Requiring seat work for long periods of time	Moving and learning most of the time
Standardized testing	Careful documentation of children's play experiences and what they reveal about their inner and outer worlds
Teacher-centered program	Child-centered program
Computers, television, the Internet	No high-tech tools—lots of multisensory experiences instead
Scheduling of "classes" into short time units	Lots of unstructured play time
Division of school day into "courses"	Frequent opportunities for serendipity, spontaneity, and fun
Creation of instructional objectives for children	Honoring the integrity, wholeness, and wisdom of young children
Requiring all students to engage in the same activities at the same time	Letting children choose their own activities

should occur in a society that is already stressed and fragmented
beyond belief is a tragedy of epic proportions.

For Further Study

1. Visit an early childhood education center in your area
that has a human development focus, and one that has an academic achievement orientation. What kinds of observations and

reflections do you have about the two programs? What advantages and disadvantages do you see with each program? Keep a record of your visits, and share your insights with a group of colleagues who have made similar visits.

2. Reflect on your own play experiences in childhood. Record any memories, feelings, and thoughts that come up as you do this. What impact did these play experiences have, if any, on your later life?

3. Observe children at free play. How do they incorporate the culture around them into their play? How do they use their imaginations? Notice the kind of social interactions that take place. What do you think that the children are learning as they play?

4. Do an Internet search on the importance of play in early childhood. Use such search terms as "play, importance," "play, positive impact," "play, positive influence," "play, creativity," and "play, cognitive skills." Have some of your colleagues engage in a similar Internet search. Come together to share your results and discuss the implications of your findings.

5. Read about Reggio Emilia schools, Waldorf schools, and developmental preschools and kindergartens. (Note: Find citations from this chapter in the References section of this book.) Engage one or more colleagues in a similar reading experience (they can either read the same sources or different sources on the same subject). If possible, visit one or more of these schools in your area. Then share your reflections and observations.

6. Ask yourself whether the early childhood programs in your local public school district tend to have a human development perspective or an academic achievement focus. What factors have contributed to this situation? If the programs are more academic, what might be done to move them toward more developmentally appropriate practices?

4

Elementary Schools: Learning How the World Works

Now, what I want is, Facts. Teach these boys and girls nothing but Facts. Facts alone are wanted in life. Plant nothing else, and root out everything else. You can only form the minds of reasoning animals upon Facts: nothing else will ever be of any service to them. This is the principle on which I bring up my own children, and this is the principle on which I bring up these children. Stick to Facts, sir!

—Mr. Gradgrind in *Hard Times*
by Charles Dickens

With the ascendancy of Academic Achievement Discourse, our nation's schools have become increasingly subject to the dictates of the Gradgrinds of education. We've returned to the "hard times" of Charles Dickens; that is to say, we've transformed too many of our classrooms into content and skills factories reminiscent of the sweat shops of the Industrial Revolution instead of making them into exciting places for the birthing of wonderful ideas. The standards movement has burdened children with a vast number of facts that must be mastered, failing which children and schools face penalties and sanctions. The cultural literacy movement has created Core Knowledge schools that give students tiny bits of lots of facts. Direct Instruction models provide teachers with rigid scripts that must be followed verbatim in order to teach children the facts of reading, writing, and math. Educational researchers use their fact-checking statistical tools to tout fact-based learning as the most scientifically rigorous teaching approach available.

In classrooms considered the best within these systems and programs, children score high on standardized exams. They assiduously learn their facts. But there is a downside. As educator Micaela Rubalcava (2004) reported:

> The children seem stressed. They twitch and jiggle their knees with nervousness, and they glance often to the round wall clock. They are 9- and 10-year-olds hunched over pencil and paper as silent as mice, performing exactly as they have been asked on pre-algebra and sentence structure. When they burst out of class for recess, lunch, and P.E. like wind-up toys, I ask a pair of boys how they like school. They say it's okay. They mention grades. They mention Accelerated Reader scores. They talk about how much work they do. They joke about getting yellow warning cards for behavior. But mostly they don't want to talk because they need to run, wiggle, and roll. A girl from the class tells me she has nothing bad to say about her current teacher, but her favorite teacher was last year. "Why did you like her so much?" I ask. "Because Mrs. X had rat bones and mummified chickens in an Egyptian shrine, and two snakes, and three turtles, and bean-bag chairs. We dissected worms and hatched trout. We journaled about the hatchlings for a long time, and on the second-to-last day of school, we freed them in a river. I got totally soaked," she giggles. (para. 6–11)

Educators who employ Academic Achievement Discourse often highlight the existence of a so-called achievement gap that has beset our nation's schools. However, there is a far more profound educational gap that needs bridging. It is the gap between the

"schoolhouse world" and the "real world." All children, but especially those at the elementary school level, have as a central developmental focus the need to find out how the world works.

As we will see in this chapter, children between the ages of 7
and 11 or 12 have unique developmental needs that make learning about the world a driving force in their lives. If their world at
school consists of rat bones, mummified chickens, snakes, and tur-
tles, then they will bend their curious minds toward these things.
If their world for 6 or 7 hours a day, 5 days a week, is the world of
tests, facts, skills, textbooks, worksheets, and commercial learning
kits, then they will turn their developmental urges toward the task
of mastering *that* particular world. Educator John Holt (1995) wrote
especially well about how school children do this. He outlined
some of the strategies that children use to make it in the traditional
classroom, including the "mumble strategy":

> The mumble strategy is particularly effective in language classes. In
> my French classes, the students used to work it on me, without my
> knowing what was going on. It is particularly effective with a teacher
> who is finicky about accents and proud of his own. To get such a
> teacher to answer his own questions is a cinch. Just make some
> mumbled, garbled, hideously un-French answer, and the teacher with
> a shudder will give the correct answer in elegant French. The student
> will have to repeat it after him, but he is out of the worst danger.
> (Holt, 1995, p. 23)

Kids learn how to read their teachers, hedge their bets, copy
their friends' homework, peek at fellow students' tests—*anything* to
survive in this high-stakes, low-excitement world.

You have to admire children for their ability to work the system. And yet, this achievement is a supreme tragedy in the making,
because children are squandering their precious energies on the
tiny postage stamp–sized world of the fact-based classroom and
are being deprived of contact with the huge, exciting, amazing real
world that's out there waiting to be discovered. As an adult learner,
you have only to imagine yourself in some real-life context to see

what kind of tragedy is unfolding here. You're engaged in a hobby, working at your job, or taking a vacation, when all of a sudden you're swooped up by some invisible educational force and made to sit at a tiny desk in a small room listening to a teacher barking out scripted lesson plans to you about your hobby, job, or trip. This, of course, is patently absurd. But why should it be any different for a child?

In the rest of this chapter, I'll examine the "schoolhouse" versus "real world" gap and show how bridging this gap is especially important for children in the elementary school years. I'll start out by looking at some of the more general developmental needs of elementary-age kids, and then focus on why *learning how the world works* is an especially important need at this time of life. Then I'll examine more closely a few of the most developmentally inappropriate practices used in elementary school that take kids away from the real world. Finally, I will look at some of the best school practices now being used that recognize children's need to explore the incredible world around them. (See Figure 4.1 for a list of appropriate and inappropriate practices at this age.)

Developmental Needs of Elementary School Kids

When children reach the age of 6 or 7, they leave the magical world of early childhood behind. No longer is the child experiencing physiognomic perceptions, synesthesia, eidetic imagery, or animism as ways of comprehending the world. Growth spurts in the brain from the ages of 6 to 13 connect brain regions that are specialized for language and understanding spatial relations (Thompson et al., 2000). No longer do kids freely mix the contents of their inner and outer experiences. Instead, they construct a *subjective* inside self and an *objective* outside world.

Piaget noted that around the age of 7 children move into concrete operational thinking. They can mentally reverse operations,

Figure 4.1

Developmentally Inappropriate and Appropriate Practices in Elementary School Education

Developmentally Inappropriate Practices	Developmentally Appropriate Practices
Artificial classroom environment	Classroom that opens out to the real world (literally and figuratively)
Overemphasis on reading, writing, and math	Reading, writing, and math in relationship to real-world discoveries
Textbooks, worksheets, and workbooks	Authentic learning materials that are normally a part of the real world (the Internet, literature, art supplies, science tools, historical artifacts, etc.)
Scripted teaching programs	Student explorations of the real world guided by the teacher
Fact-based learning programs	Learning based on encounters with the real world, resulting in ideas, insights, revelations, reflections, observations, and more

for example, adding 3 to 4 to get 7, and then taking away 3 to get 4 again. They can also conserve mass, that is, see two equivalent pieces of clay—one rolled out thin, and one clumped together in a ball—as containing the same amount of clay. They can classify objects according to their different attributes—thinness, redness, roundness, wetness—and seriate objects (e.g., sort different lengths of string) backwards and forwards (see, for example, Flavell, 1963). They can retreat into their daydreams and emerge from them into the reality of the outer world. These newly found abilities enable children to master math concepts, decode words, and think inside of their heads while they read, listen to the teacher, or engage in other learning activities.

At this age, kids can retreat into the interior of their own minds, but they also tend to take major steps out into the social world. Before 6 or 7, children live in a smaller social world, peopled largely by their parents or caregivers and a few significant peers, relatives, or teachers. Somewhere between the ages of 5 and 7, children become social beings in their own right in the midst of a larger and more complicated social network. Different cultures even have rituals that mark this entrance into the wider world. In Burma, young boys reenact the transformation of Prince Siddhartha into the Buddha in the Shinbyu ceremony. In Turkey, boys are circumcised just before entering primary school, at a time when they are able to comprehend the significance of the ritual. Jesuits have a saying: "Give me the child until he is 7, and I will show you the man." In most nonliterate cultures around the world, children begin assuming social responsibilities between 5 and 7: they start to take care of younger siblings, help hunt for game, plant seeds and harvest the crop, and engage in domestic activities such as spinning, weaving, cooking, and sewing. In modern society, children between the age of 5 and 7 move into a social world peopled not just by parents and a few significant others but also by friends, friends' siblings and parents, schoolmates, scout leaders, coaches, teammates, media heroes, and a host of other important people.

Participating fully in this social world is a big part of what this period of childhood is all about. Kids at this age are interested in discovering what the rules are for social conduct. Because they can engage in reversibility thinking, they become capable of engaging in reciprocal relationships and social rituals. When playing games, for example, they can spend as much time arguing about the rules of the game and what is fair (that is, what behaviors must be applicable to all parties involved) as they do in playing the game itself. In friendships, they engage in a give-and-take process ("I'll trade you two bubble gums for my sack lunch") or protest when the process breaks down ("You hit me and didn't say 'sorry' so I don't want to be your friend"). Life for elementary-age kids, then, is much closer to the cognitive and social dimensions of adulthood than the previous developmental stage of early childhood.

Developmental Focus: Learning How the World Works

Because children at this age are entering into active participation with a busy social world, and because they can now think for the first time in an adultlike way about the world, they become hungry to know what this world is all about. It's almost as if they are saying: "How does this big and beautiful new world work? What kinds of different people are there in it? What kinds of rules are there? What about me, how do I work? What does my heart do? Why do I breathe fast when I climb a hill? What can I achieve in this world? How fast can I run? How high can I jump? What about all these things around me that used to be part of the landscape? How do they work? How does a clock work? What makes a car run? Why is the sky blue? Why does bleach make things white? What causes lightning?"

Things that in early childhood used to inexplicably fly all over the place without the child having any mastery over them, or that simply lay beyond the young child's awareness, now become part of a new world that can be constructed, comprehended, and even controlled. "How does my bike work (so I can fix it)? How do we know what the weather will be like (so I can prepare for it)? How can I use a map (so I can find my way to a neat hiking trail)?" There is a sense of urgency and excitement about all of this. Human development expert Erik Erikson (1993) called this sensibility "industry"—the drive to discover, invent, create, and explore. It's as if the child is saying: "The world is an incredible place—there are other countries, there are people who speak different languages and who have different rules for living. There is music to listen to, and books to read, and sports to play, and nature to explore, and all kinds of other interesting things, and it's all just great!"

Children at this age are what I like to call "ecstatic pragmatists." Bring something interesting from the world into a classroom—a fossil, an African mask, a mechanical toy, an unusual-looking musical instrument, a snake or lizard (or any other living animal), and watch how kids are gaping all over each other trying to get to the object, eager to find out as much as they can about this new entry into their rapidly expanding learning universe. The importance of the kinds of discoveries that children make and the insights they have about the world at this age cannot be overstated.

Many children at this age have crystallizing experiences— experiences that seize them with a sense of wonder, excitement, or fascination, and stay with them for the rest of their lives (Walters & Gardner, 1986). When Joseph Lister, the discoverer of antiseptic surgery, was 10 years old, his father was looking over his school lessons when Joseph noticed a bubble in the glass of a window he was looking out of at the time. He observed that the bubble of glass magnified things outside, and from that time on he became fascinated with optics, eventually inventing the achromatic lens (Illingsworth & Illingsworth, 1969). The filmmaker Ingmar Bergman (1988) traced his love of the cinema back to his childhood: "I had been to the cinema for the first time and seen a film about a horse. I think it was called *Black Beauty* and was based on a famous book. The film was on at the Sture cinema and we sat in the front row of the circle. To me, it was the beginning. I was overcome with a fever that has never left me" (p. 14). After reading books in childhood about Tarzan and Dr. Doolittle (a doctor who goes to Africa and talks with animals), naturalist Jane Goodall said she began to dream of traveling to Africa (Goodall & Berman, 2000).

Once children reach the age of 6 or 7, it *is* appropriate to teach symbol systems like reading, writing, and math, because these are important aspects of this world that children are hungry to learn about. In learning how to decode squiggly lines on a page, children can imaginatively (because they now have a subjective mind) travel to outer space, China, the White House, the time of the dinosaurs, and a million other places. By learning about number systems, they can learn how the money system works and how to save for purchases of things they want to have. They can also learn about other symbol systems: systems for making art, for playing soccer, for reading music, for finding one's way across a mountain, for understanding what people from other cultures are saying. This is also an appropriate time for high-tech tools, since technology provides new windows for the child onto the wide world. Television and videotape permit the child to see life in another country without actually having to travel there, to participate in imaginative stories and adventures, and to learn new skills such as how to knit, build a table, or cook. The Internet allows even easier and quicker access to information about any aspect of the world. Computer software permits children to create their own symbolic worlds, practice skills that are valued in the world, and learn about money, rocks, history, and a thousand other things. Any learning approach that helps elementary-age children learn more about the world in which they live has legitimacy as an educational strategy.

Developmentally Inappropriate Practices at the Elementary School Level

Unfortunately, Academic Achievement Discourse has resulted in the increasing adoption of practices in the classroom that tend to significantly narrow the lens through which children gaze upon and learn about the big wide world out there. In some cases, these practices actually suppress the child's excitement about the world, and may even convince the student that she has no worth as a knowledge explorer. Erik Erikson used the term "inferiority" to describe what can happen to elementary school kids if they have their industry suppressed (1993). They cease to wonder about things, lose the zest for constructing new knowledge about the world, and no longer see themselves as positive learners. This section will detail some of the most flagrant pedagogical violations of a child's drive to learn about and master the world around him.

Overemphasis on Reading, Writing, and Math

As noted above, the teaching of reading, writing, and math is an important part of an elementary school child's initiation into the larger social world. These are powerful symbol systems that permit the child to enter into a significant engagement with the world in a new way. The question is not whether they should be taught in elementary school—of course they should—but rather to what extent they should form a part of the child's school day. *The Washington Post* (Perlstein, 2004) reported, "In recent years—particularly since the No Child Left Behind Act passed in 2001—many schools have shifted to a fervent focus on reading, writing, and math, bringing in program after program in search of what might help struggling students" (p. A1). Unfortunately, this has resulted in other school subjects being set aside. At Highland Elementary School in Wheaton, Maryland, for example, the daily hour set aside for science and social studies has been replaced with writing for 2nd and 3rd graders. Reading has been expanded to an hour and a half for all 770 of the students. Some students who are struggling with reading may spend up to half of the entire school day studying reading, Perlstein noted.

Gardner's theory of multiple intelligences (1993) criticizes schools for focusing too much attention on linguistic and logical-mathematical intelligences at the expense of the other six intelligences (musical, spatial, interpersonal, intrapersonal, bodily-kinesthetic, and naturalist). Children who possess gifts as cartoonists, animators, musicians, ecologists, violinists, woodworkers, and dancers, for example, have fewer and fewer opportunities at school (if they have any opportunities at all) to demonstrate and develop competencies that may be a key to their ultimate success and satisfaction in life (Armstrong, 1998).

An additional problem with this strong emphasis on reading, writing, and math is the significant shift in the way these subjects are taught. It wasn't so long ago when children learned to read and write by engaging in a rich interaction with the printed and spoken word through award-winning children's literature, invented spelling, significant oral language stimulation, and the teaching of specific phonetic, syntactic, and semantic skills in the context of the actual process of reading and writing in areas of interest (Goodman,

2005). These days, with the emphasis on measuring reading and writing progress through standardized testing, new reading programs have been instituted in many classrooms around the country that disconnect reading skills from the actual process of *reading in order to learn about the wider world.*

University of New Mexico professor Richard J. Meyer (2002) wrote about the shift that took place in one elementary school:

> Karen's primary classroom was a joyous place for her to teach because her district trusted her decision making about teaching and learning. Daily readers' and writers' workshops provided evidence of what children know, and Karen's use of assessments such as miscue analysis helped her decide what to teach next. Each piece of writing— and there are many in journals, stories, and other genres—suggested what children are coming to understand and what might be strengthened with the strategy lessons that Karen tailored to their needs. (para. 1)

Then, there was an outcry from the community about low reading scores at the 2nd grade level, and the school district quickly adopted and required the teaching of a systematic, direct-instruction phonics program. Meyer (2002) wrote:

> Life in the classroom changed in response to the phonics mandate because the lessons consumed time. Karen says, "My students need to hear stories. They need to be involved with real literature . . . although [now] I always feel like I'm battling the clock." She explains that the mandated program is so oriented to precision that her students are less willing to take risks as readers and writers. That, in combination with less time for writing, makes Karen wonder about all the lost possibilities: for teaching, for learning, and for young readers and writers to express themselves, their ideas, their hopes, their dreams, and their imaginations.

Clearly, in such an environment, students have far fewer opportunities to learn about the world around them. Instead, they learn what a handful of researchers, curriculum developers, and reading program publishers want them to know.

Scripted Teaching Programs

One of the key features of the phonics reading program described above is the use of "scripts" that teachers read *verbatim* as they go through each lesson plan. This increasing use of rigid scripts in teaching is largely a result of the influence of Direct Instruction (DI) on American education. Although the term "direct instruction" has been used to describe several different kinds of teaching approaches, DI was originally developed by former advertising executive Sigfried Engelmann, who in the 1960s created the DISTAR program (Direct Instruction System for Teaching Arithmetic and Reading) as part of President Johnson's War on Poverty (Engelmann, 1981). DI's recent popularity stems largely from its success as one of the top programs for improved student achievement as measured by standardized tests (American Institutes for Research, 2005).

Direct Instruction, which has its roots in the behaviorism of the 1950s (Skinner, 2002), focuses attention on making small incremental progress in mastering reading skills. To illustrate how scripts in Direct Instruction work, here is an example of a three-part script used to help students learn how to sound out the word "sat":

> 1. (Point to sat.) You're going to touch under the sounds as you sound out this word and say it fast. (Touch under s.) What's the first sound you're going to say? "sss." (Touch under a.) What's the next sound you're going to say? "aaa." (Touch under t.) What's the next sound you're going to say? "t."
> 2. Touch the first ball of the arrow. Take a deep breath and say the sounds as you touch under them. Get ready. Go. (Child touches under s, a, and t and says "sssaaat." (Repeat until firm.)
> 3. Say it fast. "sat." Yes, what word? "sat." You read the word sat. Good reading. (Engelmann, Haddox, & Bruner, 1983, p. 53)

The fact that all teachers across the country using this program are supposed to follow the same script in teaching their students means that there is a built-in standardization that lends itself well to statistical research. Its testlike atmosphere (frequent assessments are part of the DI teaching approach) means that it essentially prepares kids for the tests that will validate its method.

However, using our developmental criterion ("How well does this approach help kids learn about the world around them?"), DI and scripted lesson plans come up far short. "A trained monkey could do this program," said Janice Auld, president of the North Sacramento Education Association, when speaking about a reading program in her district based on scripted lesson plans. An experienced teacher herself, she found the process of adopting the curriculum "humiliating and demeaning" (Colt, 2005, para. 5). The lesson is disconnected from real life. Instead of learning about the word "sat" in the context of reading a book about American pioneers, the solar system, or how to cook bread, the students must learn it in the context of a boring lesson plan. What kind of robot world is *this* that they're forced to learn about?

Fact-Based Learning

Academic Achievement Discourse places a primacy on knowledge that can be assessed through standardized tests. As a result, learning programs that emphasize the acquisition of finite, testable chunks of information are those that receive the greatest support in today's Academic Achievement Discourse climate. At the forefront of this movement is the work of E. D. Hirsch Jr. (1988, 1999), who has built a pedagogical empire upon the force-feeding of factual information to school children. His Core Knowledge system of learning—a Gradgrind system for the 21st century—consists of highly structured, sequenced, factual lesson plans that require students to drill, memorize, and even experiment, draw, and sing at the command of the teacher.

At first glance, this system seems perfectly suited to the needs of elementary school children. After all, if the key developmental need at this age is to learn how the world works, then the Core Knowledge system appears to fit the bill better than any other program. Students are given a whirlwind tour through much of the world's knowledge base, from music, art, and poetry to science, mathematics, and geography. Students learn about their teeth, cell division, Islamic art, and the Civil Rights movement of the 1960s.

There are a number of problems, however, with this approach to finding out about how the world works. First it lacks genuine encounters with the *real* world. Instead, students are given their "knowledge modules" preshrunk and prewrapped. Second graders are given bags of insects to investigate (there are 16 skills they have to learn about them). Fifth graders are thrown a paper "snowball" by the teacher to learn about snow in Russia (George & Hagemeister, 2002, p. 3). Eighth graders are told to take notes on "the four things that poetry can give you" (pleasure, truth, help, involvement) (Terryn, 2002, p. 2). Lessons are structured so that the spontaneity, serendipity, and wonder that come from genuine encounters with the world are taken away and replaced with reasonable facsimiles thereof. Students are not so much finding out about the world as they are finding out about people who think they can encompass the world's richness, depth, and complexity in a series of sequenced lesson plans. They sit at their desks and have the world brought to them in little packets, instead of going out into the world and actively exploring it using their imaginations, their curiosity, and their questioning minds.

Textbooks and Worksheets

In a similar fashion, the use of commercial textbooks, worksheets, and learning systems on *any* topic, including history, social studies, science, and health, send a message to kids that the real world is somehow tightly bound up in glossy books that can't be written in and that contain lots of disconnected pictures, graphs, and sidebars. It also sends the message that the world is best interacted with by completing disposable worksheets that involve filling in the blank; circling true or false; choosing a, b, c, or d; or drawing an arrow from something in column a to something in column b. As school reformer Deborah Meier (1999–2000) put it:

> In a nation in which textbooks are the primary vehicle for distributing school knowledge, a few major textbook publishers, based on a few major state textbook laws, dominate the field, offering most teachers, schools, and students very standardized accounts of what is to be learned, and when and how to deliver this knowledge. Moreover, most textbooks have always come armed with their own end-of-chapter tests, increasingly designed to look like the real thing; indeed, test makers also are the publishers of many of the major standardized tests. (para. 50)

Textbooks hardly mirror the real world, and instead compress it into several hundred pages of colorless prose. After all, textbooks aren't written by human beings. They are written by committees anxious to avoid controversy. Education historian Diane Ravitch (2003c; see also Ravitch, 2003a) compares textbooks (which kids find boring) to equally lengthy books containing children's literature classics such as J. R. R. Tolkien's *Lord of the Rings* trilogy and the Harry Potter series (which kids find fascinating):

> In contrast to the gripping tales told by Rowling and Tolkien, our history textbooks skim lightly above the surface of events, ignoring the fact that history is first of all a story. The history books excel at mentioning vast numbers of events, people, and ideas and compressing them into short summaries of a page or two. The drama of history and biography is sacrificed to the imperative of "covering" everything in a single volume. Clashes of good and evil have been banished, replaced by pedestrian prose and thumbnail sketches. Similarly, our reading and literature books have achieved the heights of banality. Those who assemble them are careful to weed out controversial themes, anything that might upset pressure groups from left and right. They aim not to engage students' imagination but to bolster their self-esteem. Demographic correctness—the right percentage of authors and characters from every possible segment of society—has become more important than literary excellence. (para. 7–8)

In sum, the combination of a boring and rigidly presented commercially produced curriculum along with standardized testing creates a major hazard for elementary-age kids, because in such a system, they have been deprived of the one thing that they most crave at this stage of life: meaningful learning experiences that teach them about how the real world works.

The Best Elementary Schools: Examples of Developmentally Appropriate Practice

In contrast to the developmentally inappropriate educational practices I've discussed, there are an abundance of creative approaches to learning at the elementary school level that teach kids how the world works. These exemplary practices effectively bridge the gap between the artificial schoolhouse world and the richness and excitement of culture and nature. What these learning methods and programs all have in common is an educational philosophy that views the child as an active participant in constructing authentic knowledge about the world. These programs are living embodiments of Human Development Discourse insofar as they embrace a child-centered approach to learning, honor the development of the whole child, and view the highest experiences of learning in terms of meaningful and enthusiastic human interaction with the world rather than the achieving of high test scores.

MicroSociety

One unique way of teaching kids about how the world works is to reconstruct the world inside a school building. This is the central premise of the MicroSociety approach to learning, which was created by first-year Brooklyn school teacher George Richmond in 1967 in response to his "at risk" 5th grade students' lack of enthusiasm for the traditional school curriculum (Richmond, 1997). The first MicroSociety school opened in Lowell, Massachusetts, in 1981. Currently, the approach is used in more than 250 schools nationwide. In MicroSociety programs, students study traditional academic subjects in the morning, and in the afternoon apply their knowledge by constructing a minisociety within the school walls. MicroSociety schools have their own banks and economic systems (students are paid for their work and can use the "money" to buy things), governmental systems (students are tried and punished for infractions of student-created rules and laws), their own merchandising sector (students create and run their own businesses), and their own artistic and cultural institutions.

Every MicroSociety is different, as students shape their worlds according to the unique needs and interests of the student population. In one Texas school, younger students used their cash to "rent" older students to read to them. In a Florida school, a student created and marketed an exercise video. At the Lowell school, a student who wrote a series of bad checks at a Christmas auction had his wages garnished and was sentenced to community service (Wilgoren, 2001). Students at Myers Elementary School in Taylor, Michigan, have called their MicroSociety "Myersville." It includes, among other things, a boutique that sells recycled goods, a bureau of census and statistics where students conduct opinion polls and generate other relevant data about the school, a greenhouse that grows and sells seeds and plants, a museum where students teach other students about the local community, and a traffic court where students may receive a ticket for "excessive speeding" (running in the hallway) (Higgins, 2005).

Community-Based Education

Another way that children can learn about how the world works is through direct contact with their local community. Perhaps the most well-known example of this approach is the Foxfire Experiment. In 1966, Eliot Wigginton and his students at Rabun Gap–Nacoochee School in northeast Georgia embarked on a mission to interview local elders in the surrounding community and find out what they knew about the skills, traditions, experiences, and history of the Appalachian culture that they all shared. Their project gave birth to a magazine called *Foxfire* (named after the blue-green glow emitted by bioluminescent lichens that grew on decaying logs), and later to a book, a movie, a museum, and a foundation that still operates to further this kind of approach to learning in schools around the country (Wigginton, 1973). Children at Foxfire School, an elementary school in Yonkers, New York, for example, explore the nearby Hudson River and its relationship to mathematics and science. Students go on field trips that allow them to work with artists, writers, and other local experts in their trade or craft. At Tolenas Elementary School in northern California, which is situated on a section of the Suisun Marsh that once contained a Native American village, students learn about marsh ecosystems, explore how to do blacksmithing (there is a blacksmith shop nearby), and study the local history. Principal Eva LaMar reported:

> I first thought when I went to Solano County, "What history is there?" But once you start digging in and you talk to local historians, you find some of the stories. Look for old trails. Look at the geography . . . . How many quarries do you have on your land? Where did the rock from those quarries go? What monuments are in the area, or what geological aspects? Start learning about the history of [your area]. It's quite fascinating. (Ball, 2003, p. 3)

Montessori Schools

While Maria Montessori's educational philosophy is most frequently associated with early childhood education, she also laid the foundations for her method to be use with older students (see, for example, Montessori, 1984). At the elementary school level, the Montessori method focuses a great deal of attention on helping kids learn about how the world works. They explore nature with binoculars, magnifiers, and bug "relocators." They learn about other cultures by investigating their architecture, music, flags, and customs. They use hands-on materials to learn concepts in algebra, geometry, physics, chemistry, biology, and other subjects that aren't usually covered until high school in most other school systems. They study the great composers and artists of the world, investigate origami and Japanese calligraphy, put together geography puzzles, and use self-correcting manipulative materials to learn about everything from mammals and sacred places to outer space and fungi. But unlike the Core Knowledge curriculum, where teachers execute highly directive lesson plans run on tight schedules, students in Montessori elementary schools have several hours a day to explore and investigate the world without teacher control or coercion. They choose the activities they want to study and spend as much time as they need to acquire skills and knowledge about the world. "We don't use textbooks," says Phillip Dosmann, principal of Craig Montessori Elementary School in the Milwaukee Public School District. "We spend a lot of time preparing the environment so kids will learn to make good choices about how to spend their time" (Carr, 2003, para. 15). Currently, there are an estimated 250 public schools that have adopted the Montessori method in the United States.

School Partnerships with Children's Museums

Children's museums immerse students in highly stimulating and highly interactive environments that engage them in learning about other cultures, ecology, science, mechanics, and many other subjects through direct contact with authentic materials under the guidance of experts trained to facilitate their discoveries. The first children's museum in the world was founded in 1899 in Brooklyn, New York. However, only since the 1960s and 1970s have museums for children become a regular part of the urban landscape in many cities.

Today there are more than 300 children's museums in the United States. Increasingly, these museums are forming alliances with public schools so that curriculum can be tied directly to museum exhibits. The Weaving Resources program at the Minnesota Children's Museum, for example, provides every St. Paul school child from kindergarten through 2nd grade with a series of in-depth educational experiences based on the museum's exhibitions and programs. First-grade students spend six weeks studying insects using the museum's Insect Discovery Kit, and then take a trip to the museum's Anthill exhibit. Second graders focus on social studies and use the museum's One World gallery as a focus for their explorations (Association of Children's Museums, 2003). The Opal School in Portland, Oregon, is a charter school of the Portland Public Schools and a program of the Portland Children's Museum. Groups or individuals at Opal have initiated projects in conjunction with the museum that have led to inquiry about insects, writing and performing a screenplay, reading original poetry in public settings, and designing a weather station. "Nobody flunks museums," said Frank Oppenheimer, who founded the Exploratorium in San Francisco, which also conducts a number of programs in coordination with area public schools (as cited in Brandt, 1993, p. 6).

Harvard psychologist Howard Gardner has been a leading advocate for the use of children's museums as a model of learning for students:

> When I talk about children's museums, what I mean is that kids did not evolve to sit still for 40 hours a week, not being allowed to talk to anybody else, and simply have to listen to lectures, or read from a text, and fill in worksheets. In a children's museum, kids have an opportunity to work with very interesting kinds of things, at their own pace, in their own way, in my terms, using the kinds of intelligence which they're strong in. If they've learned some concepts in school, they can try them out at the very interesting kinds of displays at the museum. If the museum raises questions for them that they can't answer, they can bring them back to school, or to parents, or to the library or somewhere. I was really convinced by the power of children's museums when I found that there were certain kids who could sit in school for weeks and you couldn't tell anything about them, but you put them in a children's museum for a day or two (or an exploratorium or science museum), and you learn about those kids, and how they learn and what's important, and how they go about solving problems. (1994)

At children's museums kids learn how the world works through direct exploration, open-ended inquiry, and hands-on projects.

There are thousands of other elementary schools around the country using methods that engage children in authentic interactions with the real world. These approaches include the following:

- **Project-based learning.** Students focus on a specific topic and develop an exhibition, presentation, or product that illustrates their learning (for example, a science fair project that explores water pollution in the community) (see, for example, Blumenfeld et al., 1991).

- **Integrated thematic instruction.** Teachers and students choose a theme (such as the seasons, inventions, our neighborhood, or ecological awareness) and together create a curriculum (activities, projects, and resources) that explores the theme in depth (see, for example, Kovalik, 1993).

- **Interdisciplinary studies.** Teachers team together from different subject areas and develop a common curriculum around a central focus (for example, "the life cycle" might be approached in terms of cycles of history, the life cycle of a butterfly, how other cultures ritualize significant events in the human life cycle, and the theme of the human life cycle in literature) (see, for example, Jones, Rasmussen, & Moffitt, 1997).

- **Multiple intelligences curricula.** Students take courses in a variety of subjects that engage all eight of their intelligences in real-world avocations (for example, courses in architecture, landscaping, musical composition, yoga, rock collecting, or publishing) (see, for example, Armstrong, 2000b).

- **Simulated classrooms.** An entire classroom is turned into a rocket ship, a medieval castle, a rain forest, or some other aspect of the real world, and students engage in activities designed to teach science, history, ecology, and other subjects within that living context (Taylor & Walford, 1972).

Even traditional school activities such as field trips, career days, and terrariums serve to get students out of the classroom or alternatively to bring aspects of the real world into the school. Each elementary school, of course, will find different ways of bridging the "reality gap" between school and life. However, the heart of this endeavor consists of throwing off inappropriate practices (textbooks, worksheets, scripts, drills, etc.) and seeking ways in which children—hungry for interaction with the real world—can have their developmental needs met in a significant way.

For Further Study

1. Visit an elementary school that uses academic practices such as Direct Instruction, Core Knowledge, textbooks, or frequent use of testing. Then visit an elementary school that uses developmental practices such as MicroSociety, museum partnerships, multiple intelligences, or community-based education. Compare your experiences of visiting each school. What did you notice about the emotional atmosphere at each school? To what extent was there genuine excitement for learning at each school? To what extent did you feel that students were learning about how the world works? Discuss your observations with colleagues who have visited the same or similar schools.

2. Think back to your own experiences in elementary school. Remember teachers who in retrospect seemed to primarily embrace a human development perspective in their classroom and those who were primarily focused on academic achievement. Which teachers did you prefer? Which teachers seemed to teach you more? How do you feel the educational climate in contemporary culture has changed from when you were an elementary school student with respect to human development and academic achievement?

3. Observe elementary school children engaged in formal and informal learning experiences (in and out of school). Do they seem

interested in learning about how the world works? If so, what aspects of the world do they seem most interested in learning about? How does the environment they're in at the time either support or not support their curiosity about the world?

4. Find out more about one of the developmentally appropriate practices described in this chapter (by using the Internet, reading, school visits, professional development, etc.). Implement some aspect of this practice into your current school setting if appropriate. Keep a record of the process of implementation, including students' initial reactions, the quality of their involvement (emotionally, cognitively, and creatively), and their own evaluations of the practices some time after the initial implementation of the practice.

5

Middle Schools:
Social, Emotional,
and Metacognitive Growth

In July of 1963, William Alexander, chairman of the department of education at George Peabody College, was on his way to deliver an address at Cornell University on the successes of the junior high school movement when his flight was delayed at LaGuardia Airport in New York City. Because he had nothing else to do while waiting for his flight, he reviewed his speech and decided that it needed rewriting. Starting with the presentation he had planned to give—a fairly conventional talk on junior high school—he used the several-hour layover to write a new speech that called for substantial reforms in the education of young teens. Criticizing the junior high school format as merely a "junior" version of high school, he suggested changes that would take into consideration the special developmental needs of early adolescence. He argued that there should be a unique institution that would meet those needs: an intermediate or "middle" school between elementary school and high school. The speech that Alexander ultimately gave at Cornell

was the beginning of the middle school movement in America
(Alexander, 1995). The number of middle schools—schools geared
for students from 11 to 15 years of age—increased from 2,080 in
1970 to 10,944 in 1998 and to almost 12,000 by 2001–2002 (National
Association of Elementary School Principals, 2004; Zepeda & Mayers, 2002).

The emergence of the middle school movement in the 1960s
represented a milestone in the history of Human Development Discourse. This movement recognized that young adolescents are not
simply older elementary school students nor younger high school
students, but that there are dramatic changes that occur during
this time of life requiring a radically different and unique approach
to education. Middle school educators understood that the biological event of puberty fundamentally disrupts the relatively smooth
development of the elementary school years and has a profound
impact upon the cognitive, social, and emotional lives of young
teens. In line with this important insight, they saw the need for
the provision of special instructional, curricular, and administrative changes in the way that education takes place for kids in early
adolescence. Among those changes were the establishment of a
mentor relationship between teacher and student, the creation of
small communities of learners, and the implementation of a flexible
interdisciplinary curriculum that encourages active and personalized learning.

Regrettably, the rise of Academic Achievement Discourse over
the past few years threatens to undermine these reforms. Citing,
among other things, poor standardized test results, a recent Rand
Corporation report challenged the rationale for having separate
middle schools, noting that "research suggests that the onset of
puberty is an especially poor reason for beginning a new phase of
schooling" (Juvonen, Le, Kaganoff, Augustine, & Constant, 2004,
pp. 18–19). The Thomas B. Fordham Institute report *Mayhem in
the Middle,* which was critical of middle schools, defined "middle-
schoolism" as "an approach to educating children in the middle

grades (usually grades 5–8), popularized in the latter half of the 20th century, that contributed to a precipitous decline in academic achievement among American early adolescents" (Yeche, 2005, p. i). Many large school districts, including those in Cincinnati, Cleveland, Minneapolis, Philadelphia, Memphis, and Baltimore, are now in the process of reconfiguring their schools away from the middle school model and toward a K–8 format (Wallis, Miranda, & Rubiner, 2005).

The enactment of the No Child Left Behind Act certainly is part of the reason for the abandonment of the middle school philosophy in recent years. "The big issue is NCLB doesn't take into account the unique needs of middle schools," noted Steven van Zandt, principal of Aviara Oaks Middle School in Carlsbad, California. "NCLB doesn't address any sort of developmental needs of middle school students at all" (Association of California School Administrators, 2003). NCLB is essentially nondevelopmental for *all* levels of education. It requires uniformly high test scores throughout the K–12 curriculum without regard to developmental changes at different stages of childhood and adolescence.

This is a fundamental mistake. Middle schools, or something very much like them, are needed to provide students in early adolescence with an environment that can help them negotiate the impact of puberty on their intellectual, social, and emotional lives. Educators need to understand the developmental needs of young adolescents, and in particular their neurological, social, emotional, and metacognitive growth. Some of these developmental needs are ignored or subverted by inappropriate educational practices such as fragmented curricula, large impersonal schools, and lesson plans that lack vitality. Practices at the best schools honor the developmental uniqueness of young adolescents, including the provision of a safe school environment, student-initiated learning, student roles in decision making, and strong adult role models (see Figure 5.1 for a more complete list).

Figure 5.1

Developmentally Inappropriate and Appropriate Practices in Middle School or Junior High School

Developmentally Inappropriate Practices	Developmentally Appropriate Practices
Unsafe school climate	Safe school climate
Large, impersonal schools	Small learning communities
Impersonal adult interactions	Personal adult relationships
Fragmented curriculum	Engaged learning
Negative role models or no role models	Positive role models
Metacognitive strategies limited to math and reading	Metacognitive strategies integrated into all courses
No significant arts program	Expressive arts activities for all students
No meaningful health and wellness program	Health and wellness focus
Emotionally flat learning experiences	Emotionally meaningful curriculum
Teacher- and administrator-controlled learning environment	Student roles in decision making
Student voices not listened to or respected	Honoring and respecting student voices
Total focus on academic learning to the neglect of social and emotional development	Facilitating social and emotional growth

Developmental Needs of Early Adolescence

Although it's clear that children going through puberty (average age 10½ for girls and 11½ to 12 for boys) are still years away from procreating in our complex contemporary society, as far as nature is concerned they're ready to breed at any time. One of the most important aspects of early adolescence that tends to be overlooked by educators is that millions of years of evolution have been spent making sure that the reproductive systems of young teens develop normally and are in good working order so that the species can continue to replicate itself. As far as nature is concerned, this is the most important thing that can happen in the entire life of an individual organism or species. Consequently, when we address the subject of young adolescents—with their mood swings, their impulsivity, their rebelliousness, their irritability, and their other troubles—we must always keep in the back of our minds the knowledge that the hormonal, neurological, and physical changes that give rise to these "problems" in puberty take place because the body, emotions, and mind are being prepared biologically for this incredibly complex, delicate, and all-important evolutionary task. This doesn't make our job any easier as educators, but at least it sets the context for beginning to approach the matter of understanding early adolescent development and how best to create an educational environment that will optimally help young teens generate *not* children, aggression, or pathos but creative ideas, positive projects, and proactive contributions to the society of which they are becoming an increasingly integral part.

Having said this, we can now turn to the changes themselves. Puberty occurs when a gene, ironically named KiSS-1, triggers the hypothalamus to secrete a substance called gonadotropin-releasing hormone (GRH), which stimulates the pituitary gland to release two forms of gonadotropin: luteinizing hormone and follicle-stimulating hormone. These chemicals in turn trigger the production of male sex hormones like testosterone that promote male sex characteristics and initiate sperm production, and female sex hormones (estrogens) that promote female sex characteristics and start the menstrual cycle. Contrary to popular belief, it is not so much the direct influence of hormones on the body that is associated with the emotional turbulence of puberty. Rather, it is the impact that these hormones have on the development of the brain (Sisk & Foster, 2004). Surges of testosterone at puberty, for example, swell the amygdala, an almond-shaped part of the limbic system (emotional brain) that generates feelings of fear and anger (Giedd et al., 1996). Similarly, estrogen seems to affect serotonin levels at puberty, accounting for higher rates of depression among teenage girls (Born, Shea, & Steiner, 2002). Gonadal hormones in both sexes may account at least in part for a surge in gray matter in the frontal, parietal, and temporal lobes of the neocortex shortly before puberty, followed by a decline thereafter (Giedd et al., 1999). It remains to be seen whether there is a relationship between this pre-pubertal spike and the initiation of Piaget's cognitive stage of formal operational thinking, which begins around the same time (Flavell, 1963).

Overall, though, early adolescence presents a neurological picture that involves a relatively developed *limbic* system or emotional brain coexisting with a relatively *underdeveloped* prefrontal cortex. The prefrontal cortex is the part of the brain that controls executive functions like inhibition of impulses, reflection, and planning (Giedd, 2004). To put it another way, young teens' brains have their accelerators pressed all the way to the floor, while their brakes have yet to be installed.

What all this means is that the biggest need for young adolescents in education is not getting higher test scores but rather learning how to direct those surging emotional impulses into productive channels, learning how to transmute the drive for mate-seeking into positive social relationships, and learning how to mobilize their newly developed metacognitive abilities in the service of reflecting on and modulating the transformations that are taking place in their bodies and minds. Erik Erikson (1993) saw adolescence as the time of identity formation. Dolls, stamp collections, and praise from the teacher no longer have the panache that they did in earlier years. Instead, in the midst of a raging surge of neuropeptides, young adolescents are struggling to find out who they really are. They do this, according to Erikson, by essentially bouncing their provisional identities off significant others in their midst—groups, gangs, cliques, girlfriends and boyfriends, heroes, and villains—and seeing what sticks. Consequently, adolescence is an intensely social time, when the hunger for belonging, community, social status, and emotional closeness provide the context within which teens discover their identity. Failing this, they risk falling into what Erikson called *role diffusion* or the development of a negative identity such as "addict," "gangbanger," "slut," "doper," "dealer," or all-around "loser."

For thousands of years, cultures have known about the perils and promises of puberty and have organized special educational interventions at this time. They have developed rites of passage as a means of mobilizing the intense changes taking place during puberty so that these changes may take place not in disorder but in the service of the community into which they are entering (see Eliade, 1994; van Gennep, 1961). By our modern standards, these rites of passage do not pass muster. Many of them were brutal and even fatal for those who failed to survive their rigors. Boys might be placed in a pit and starved for days or engage in other endurance feats. Girls might be secluded in a hut for weeks, or taken off into the ocean and told to swim back to shore. Despite the bizarre (to our contemporary society) nature of many of these rites, one still has to appreciate the ingenuity of these cultures for finding ways in which to take boys and girls and turn them into mature men and women.

One of the tragedies of contemporary life is that no fully developed rites of passage exist for taking adolescents from childhood to adulthood. As a result, many adolescents try to create their own rites of passage through drug experimentation, highway thrills, sexual risk taking, gang violence, binge drinking, or other dangerous activities that serve to separate them from childhood but that do not, alas, manage to incorporate them into the community of mature adults. Although the schools cannot be expected to take full responsibility for this vital role of helping adolescents make the passage into adulthood, they *absolutely must* design their educational practices with these considerations in mind. Schools need to face the reality of puberty head-on and create approaches to learning that engage the social, emotional, and metacognitive dimensions of young adolescence so that these aspects of the self may be allowed to blossom over time into full-bodied maturity.

Inappropriate Developmental Practices in Middle Schools

One of the biggest problems with the recent abandonment of middle schools by school districts around the country is that the entire middle school philosophy is being rejected in reaction to poorly planned middle school experiments that simply didn't work out. When one looks at these failed middle schools, it becomes apparent that most of them failed because they did not reflect the features of good middle schools in the first place. They were often large, overcrowded, unsafe, impersonal places that called themselves middle schools simply because they served students in the middle grades.

Similarly shortsighted is the idea that the problems of early adolescence can be solved simply by putting 7th and 8th graders back in elementary school. The danger here is that teens will be "administratively relocated" without having their unique developmental needs addressed. A final problem that only compounds the difficulty in creating middle schools that meet the real needs of early adolescence is the role that Academic Achievement Discourse has had in the passage of laws such as the No Child Left Behind Act. Between 2003 and 2005, the number of middle schools identified as "needing improvement" under this law more than doubled. In the school year 2004–2005, 36 percent of all Title I middle schools were identified for improvement (Center on Education Policy, 2005). In response to NCLB, middle schools have increased the amount of class time devoted to direct instruction and decreased the time available for electives. In some cases, student advisory periods set aside for students to speak with teachers or counselors about their personal needs and academic concerns have been turned into test-prep periods (Lounsbury & Vars, 2003). These trends continue to depersonalize the school climate for students at a time when they need personalized treatment more than ever. Here are a few of the educational practices that are most damaging to students in middle schools:

Large, Impersonal Schools. As noted above, some indigenous cultures have intuitively understood the precarious nature of puberty and have devised carefully planned environments within which the dangerous aspects of puberty can be safely navigated to help the adolescent cross the bridge into maturity. Throwing a student into a large and impersonal middle school environment does not show much thought or sensitivity with regard to this important responsibility. "Good large middle schools are an oxymoron," wrote Theodore Sizer in his book *Horace's Hope*. "Managers who in the name of efficiency pack hundreds of awkward, often frightened preteens into massive buildings forget what a crowd means to an 11 year old, particularly if most of the other people there, both kids and adults, are total strangers and often speak a different language. Efficiency, one wonders, of what sort and for whom?" (Sizer, 1997a, p. 30). Large middle schools are more likely to use substitute teachers to fill teaching vacancies than small or medium-sized schools, thus adding to the impersonal climate (Texas Center for Educational Research, 2001). Moreover, teachers at large middle schools are less likely to collaborate, use innovative teaching approaches, or personalize instruction to meet students' needs (Wasley et al., 2000).

Unsafe School Climate. Entering puberty is difficult enough without having to endure school environments that threaten young teens with bullying, name calling, drugs, and violence. These kinds of negative experiences are poisons that interact insidiously with young adolescents' delicate neurological and emotional makeup and threaten to create negative behavior patterns that will haunt them for the rest of their lives. Of paramount importance in the construction of an optimal school climate is the elimination of these types of negative influences and the provision of a safe and protected school environment within which adolescents can flourish. Yet a study of one Midwestern middle school revealed that 80 percent of students admitted to engaging in physical aggression, social ridicule, teasing, name calling, and issuing threats within the previous 30 days (CNN, 1999). Eighty-seven percent of middle schools report at least one incident of violence, and almost 30 percent report at least one *serious* incidence of violence in the previous year (National Center for Education Statistics, 2003).

Fragmented Curriculum. One of the problems with current emphasis on academic content and skills at the middle school level is that students are required to meet hundreds of standards that ultimately threaten to overwhelm them in a sea of paperwork and meaningless assignments. One study of Texas middle school principals noted that 88 percent of the principals said that "nearly all" of their teachers incorporated TEKS, or the Texas Essential Knowledge and Skills, into their lesson plans (Texas Center for Educational Research, 2001). As noted in the Carnegie report *Turning Points 2000: Educating Adolescents in the 21st Century*:

> One common complaint is that the sheer number of standards some states and school districts require makes it impossible for a school to attend to every one of them. Taken together, such mandated standards in the disciplines, or even within a single discipline, may require more time for teaching, learning, and assessment than any school could ever hope to provide. Teachers' and administrators' concerns about "covering" everything that the standards apparently demand often tie directly to their concern (or fear) about being held accountable for "a little bit about everything." Coverage means touching on many topics or facts in a shallow fashion (to wit, the American textbook). On a test covering a myriad of topics, students are hard-pressed to recall facts presented in isolation, devoid of meaning or connection, and teachers are held accountable for the inevitably highly variable performance. (Jackson & Davis, 2000, para. 9)

Moreover, textbooks are often inaccurate, misleading, or incomplete in their treatment of math, science, history, literature, and other subjects (see, for example, Loewen, 1996). Adrift in a sea of irrelevant content, young teens are deprived of the opportunity to engage in focused learning adventures that can help them develop their identities, sharpen their metacognitive minds, and channel their burgeoning energies.

Emotionally Flat Learning Experiences. Individuals going through early adolescence are particularly sensitive to the presence or absence of *emotion* in their classroom learning experiences. If they are required to learn in classrooms that largely emphasize lecture, textbooks, written assignments, and tests, their own motivation is likely to wane. And yet, as noted above, NCLB and other pressures to conform to Academic Achievement Discourse are making these kinds of environments far more common in middle schools.

In one study of middle school students' perceptions of learning experiences, most students reported that active learning motivated them more often than lecture, overhead, or textbook learning. One student, for example, reported his feelings on hearing his teacher say, "Open your textbooks to page 189": "Well, I feel that when I'm working in a group and not in the textbooks that I learn the most—'cause the textbooks—some people, they don't follow it. They put stuff in words and ways that you can't really understand it" (para. 14). Another student responded to an overhead lesson plan by saying: "We hardly had anything to do. We were just getting told all of our information. It's all lectures. You'd come in here and you did no work. You'd just sit there and some people would say, 'Oh, it's a really easy class.' Yeah, it's an easy class because it's so boring" (Bishop & Pflaum, 2005, para. 18). These are not the kind of learning experiences to give to a student whose biological system is shouting at him, "It's time to move out into the world!"

The Best Middle Schools: Examples of Developmentally Appropriate Educational Practices

What we know about early adolescents and their neurological, social, emotional, and intellectual growth provides us with solid guidelines in structuring optimal middle schools. Of paramount importance in this reform effort is the use of Human Development Discourse, not Academic Achievement Discourse, in developing methods, strategies, programs, and environments for young teens. As long as educators continue to look to high test scores, tough standards, and heavy academic content as a solution to middle school woes, they will be fundamentally unprepared to help young teens make the transition to maturity. What follows is a list of 12 key features that must be a part of any authentic, developmentally appropriate plan for reforming middle schools.

Safe School Climate

The most important factor in meeting the needs of young adolescents in school is a safe school climate. As Abraham Maslow (1987) wisely observed, if people are struggling to meet their basic physiological and safety needs, there is no energy left for meeting their higher needs of love, belonging, esteem, and self-actualization. Zero-tolerance policies are not the solution for making schools safe. They may work in the short run by suspending troublemakers, but they leave the underlying problems of violence untouched (The Civil Rights Project at Harvard University, 2000).

Instead, schools need to create positive interventions that get at the root of the difficulty, including anti-bullying programs, conflict resolution, character education, gang awareness, alcohol and drug abuse counseling, student court, peer mediation, and anger management. At Lewis Middle School in Paso Robles, California, students tutor kids academically, mediate conflicts, and mingle with shy 6th graders who are having difficulty making the transition from elementary school. "Students are often able to identify problems before adults can," Principal Richard Oyler said (Wilson, 2005). Students focus on the Value of the Month at Sparrows Point Middle School in Baltimore. During the month, they engage in lesson plans, listen to guest speakers, and study material that emphasizes such values as responsibility, respect, tolerance, compassion, or honesty. Clubs at Sparrows Point such as Students Against Destructive Decisions and Future Educators of America have incorporated the monthly values into their projects, and the school has engaged in a Pitch In for Progress campaign that raises money for worthy causes. In the past two years, the school has seen a sharp drop in suspensions and an increase in attendance and in the number of students on the honor roll (Ruddle, 2005). By working to solve the underlying causes of violence, middle schools can ensure that students will not only learn in safe environments but will also become proactive members of society.

Small Learning Communities

A large body of research supports—and demands—the implementation of small school environments at the middle level. Small schools have fewer instances of theft, assaults, and vandalism than large schools (DeVoe et al., 2002). They experience lower dropout rates and increased levels of motivation and learning success (Cotton, 2001). They provide students with a shelter from the storm, so to speak, to enable them to focus on learning and become successful students.

School reformers Thomas Sergiovanni and Deborah Meier recommend no more than 300 students per school, but others believe that middle schools with as many as 700 students can maintain a small school environment (Molnar, 2002). The Talent Development Middle Schools project at Johns Hopkins University focuses on establishing learning communities of 200 to 300, with two or three teachers responsible for no more than 100 students (Herlihy & Kemple, 2004). Having a large middle school campus is no deterrent to creating small communities. Creekland Middle School in Laurenceville, Georgia, has almost 3,000 students, but it is structured into five communities, each with its own administrative staff. Students are assigned to a community in 6th grade and stay there until they leave for high school. Teachers work in teams of two so they can get to know the students better (Jacobsen, 2000). Through creative administrative and funding strategies, any middle school environment can be structured according to a "small is beautiful" ethos.

Personal Adult Relationships

Coming of age in the 21st century is a difficult prospect for many kids who have little contact even with their own parents. According to researcher Mihaly Csikszentmihalyi (2000): "Most of the time, adolescents are either alone (26%) or with friends (34%) and classmates (19%). Very little time is spent in the company of adults. The typical American adolescent spends only about five minutes a day alone with his or her father—not nearly enough to transmit the wisdom and values that are necessary for the continuation of a civil society" (p. 46). Middle schools and junior high schools that shuttle kids from one teacher to the next every 42 minutes are only making the problem worse.

On the other hand, providing a student with one teacher who serves as an advisor, mentor, counselor, or guide can be instrumental for some kids to help them feel a sense of safety, confidence, and purpose in their learning. Exemplary middle schools assign students to homeroom teachers or advisor–teachers who are with them during their entire journey through the middle grades. At Abraham Lincoln Middle School in Gainesville, Florida, advisors are assigned to 18–22 students for their entire three years at Lincoln. Advisors mentor their charges, serve as advocates for the students, and start the day with rituals that include student sharing (Doda, 2002). Good middle schools use looping, a procedure that keeps students with one or more teachers over a period of two or more years. "Humans need meaningful relationships, particularly when they are in major developmental periods," said John H. Lounsbury, dean emeritus of the School of Education at Georgia College & State University. "So many of the important objectives of education cannot be effectively achieved in a short-term relationship" (Ullman, 2005, para. 2).

Engaged Learning

An observation that has been consistently noted about young adolescents is their decreased motivation for learning compared to kids in the elementary school years. This has traditionally been ascribed to the physiological and emotional changes going on inside them. However, it may be more apt to suggest that it is the quality of the learning environment that in large part determines whether they will be engaged in their studies (Anderman & Midgley, 1998). If a student enters a large, impersonal system where he or she is told exactly what to learn, read, study, and memorize, then it is likely that the student will not be motivated. On the other hand, if the student is given a significant role in determining the kinds of learning experiences he or she will have, then the burgeoning energies of adolescence will only fuel the motivation to learn. Seventh graders at Helen King Middle School in Portland, Maine, have produced a CD-ROM about Maine's endangered species. At Harry Hurt Middle School in Destrehan, Louisiana, students take part in a program called the Wetland Watcher, which involves monitoring water quality, planting trees to halt coastal erosion, and educating others about the importance of taking care of the environment (Ball, 2004). Students at Martin Luther King Jr. Middle School in Berkeley, California, prepare and eat their own organically grown lunches from their own gardens (Furger, 2004a). In each of these cases, students are engaged directly in real-life pursuits rather than artificially contrived lesson plans that have little or no relevance to their lives.

Positive Role Models

Perhaps the most critical element in the ancient rites of passage was the presence of mature individuals to help adolescents make the transition into full membership in the society. As noted above, this factor is often missing from the lives of young teens. Middle schools need to be places where a student will have contact with older people who have vital lives of their own and who are themselves authentic human beings. There are many middle school programs where this is a focus. Eyes to the Future, for example, is a National Science Foundation–sponsored program that pairs 7th and 8th grade students with high school girls and women mentors working in science, math, and technology. Math Understanding through the Science of Life brings together Duke University engineering students and middle school students to study worms, predict the weather, and engage in other projects that apply mathematics to the real world (Dickinson, 2001). There are many other ways in which middle schools can expose their students to positive role models. Parent volunteers can offer their services as experts in specific fields. Outside experts can be engaged to share their findings with students. The school can offer a program of positive role models in the curriculum to study the lives of famous individuals who overcame adversity, or successful individuals in the community who come in and talk about what helped them achieve success. The Role Model Program in San Jose, California, for example, brings business and community leaders into Santa Clara County classrooms to encourage positive life choices and educational achievement. In these and other ways, middle school educators can help to counteract much of the negative influence young teens receive from tainted media heroes, celebrated gang leaders, and other damaged individuals who never quite made the journey into maturity.

Metacognitive Strategies

Students entering the emotional turmoil of adolescence are going through a major shift in their ability to think. They are entering the formal operational stage of cognitive development. Now, for the first time, they can think about thinking itself. They can stand above themselves and look down and reflect on what they're doing. This capacity is an important resource for adolescents who have their foot on the gas pedal before their brakes have been fully installed. Instead of acting on impulse, the mind can be trained to observe what's going on and to take appropriate measures. Typically, educators steeped in Academic Achievement Discourse have jumped on formal operations in adolescence as a justification to teach students in the middle grades pre-algebra or algebra. This is an oversimplification of this important resource of the mind.

Students should be helped to use their new kind of mind in learning study skills, reflecting on curriculum materials, exploring the nature of conflicts in their lives, and setting realistic goals for themselves. At Knotty Oak Middle School in Coventry, Kentucky, students are taught how to unpack any text by accessing what they already know about the topic, visualizing the material, and hunting down material in the text from which they can draw specific conclusions. "Learning is messy," says English Department Chairwoman Constance Tundis. "I tell my kids I want to see wood burning. I want to see five crossouts because that means you're thinking five times more deeply. It's all about asking questions and not looking for answers. If they know what to attack, what to look for, how to connect, they'll find the right answers" (Steiny, 2005, para. 17). Harvard Project Zero's Practical Intelligence for School project has prepared materials to guide middle school students in creating their own approaches to studying, planning, reflecting, and coping with the many demands of school and schoolwork (Blythe, White, & Gardner, 1995; Williams, Blythe, White et al., 1996). Similarly, with conflict resolution, students can be helped to step outside of themselves long enough to look at the social or emotional difficulties they find themselves in and seek positive solutions to resolving them.

Expressive Arts Activities

Given all of the emotional and physical tumolt rolling inside of young adolescents, it's a wonder that more focus has not been placed on the expressive arts at the middle school level. Expressive arts should be considered *a core component* of any middle school plan. The arts provide opportunities for young teens to express themselves in an atmosphere that is *without judgment* in areas such as sculpture, painting, drama, music, and dance. It's virtually impossible to fail in the expressive arts. In the course of expressing themselves artistically, students can sublimate sexual energies, channel violent impulses, sort out emotional conflicts, and build a deeper sense of identity. These are all critical developmental tasks in early adolescence.

At Clarkson School of Discovery, a public magnet middle school in Bladen County, North Carolina, students read children's literature and then develop the characters through creative movement. They also construct "heirlooms," or books that they want to keep for the rest of their lives, using photography, art, and language. At Hand Middle School in Columbia, South Carolina, students write poems and fiction about weather patterns and take on the roles of famous poets during the Harlem Renaissance (Stevenson & Deasy, 2005). Young adolescents should have the opportunity to do some type of creative art activity *every day,* whether it is integrated into the regular curriculum as above or engaged in as a freestanding activity. When young teens write poems, work in clay, draw, paint, dance, and sing, they are creatively involved in the act of forming themselves as autonomous individuals. The benefit to society could not be greater.

Health and Wellness Focus

As students' bodies change during puberty, somebody needs to be around to help them understand what's happening to them. A recent poll by National Public Radio, the Kaiser Family Foundation, and Harvard's Kennedy School of Government indicates that only 7 percent of Americans say sex education should not be taught in the schools (Henry J. Kaiser Family Foundation, 2004). Sex education should be only a part of a larger effort to inform young adolescents about issues relevant to their lives such as substance abuse, depression, eating disorders, and other ills that can begin at this stage of development. Moreover, all of this should be done within a context that emphasizes how to stay healthy, rather than how to avoid disease. At Madison Junior High in Naperville, Illinois, students wear heart monitors during their weekly 12-minute run and use a comprehensive computer-based fitness station that measures everything from strength and flexibility to cholesterol levels (Furger, 2001). Health courses in middle schools at Parsipanny–Troy Hills School District in New Jersey cover everything from stress management and sexually transmitted diseases to substance abuse and pregnancy and childbirth. By not shying away from sensitive subjects that are critical to the lives of young adolescents, middle school educators can show that they are really tuned in to the lives of their students.

Emotionally Meaningful Curriculum

Given that the limbic system or "emotional brain" is particularly active during early adolescence, it seems clear that the curriculum needs to be built around topics and themes that have emotional content and that engage students' feelings in a gripping way. Yet, as noted above, much of the curriculum in middle schools is textbook-based (read: *bo*-ring) and aligned to standards that may sound good to the politicians who enacted them into law but fall far short of reaching the real worlds of passionate teenagers.

Exemplary middle schools teach history, social studies, literature, science, and even math in ways that have an impact on the emotional lives of young teens. At Benjamin Franklin Middle School in Ridgewood, New Jersey, for example, students read about the Warsaw Ghetto and then discuss how they can combat injustices that they see in their own lives. In another class, students reflect in their journals on what it must feel like to be a foster child (Curtis, 2001a). Science students at Central Middle School in Quincy, Massachusetts, study genetics by creating family trees and examining the appearance of traits such as musical ability in their genealogy (Harvard Project Zero, 2006).

Whatever the lesson might be, teachers should always attempt to link it in some way to the feelings, memories, or personal associations of the students. A simple strategy might be to ask students to "think of a time in your life when you . . . ." If the topic is the American Revolution, students might think of examples of revolution in their own lives. If the topic is the central problem of a character in a novel, they might think of similar problems they faced in the past. Any time teachers can connect the curriculum to young adolescents' limbic systems, and then link those emotions to metacognitive reflections ("How would you handle the problem differently now?"), they are teaching in a developmentally appropriate way for this level.

Student Roles in Decision Making

Although student-initiated learning is an important component of good middle schools, students must also have a wider role to play in the affairs of the school. They should be involved in maintaining discipline through teen court, shaping school assemblies or special events, and providing meaningful feedback about courses, the school environment, and other aspects of running the school. They should have an opportunity to express their ideas and feelings in a democratic context in the classroom. It seems rather strange to me that we expect students to learn about democracy in school climates that are more often run like dictatorships! Students at Webb Middle School in Austin, Texas, participate in shared decision making through class meetings. At one meeting, for example, a student shared his concerns about hallway safety and suggested a hall monitor system that was embraced by his classmates and implemented as school policy (Appelsies & Fairbanks, 1997). Talent Middle School students in Talent, Oregon, lead parent–teacher conferences (Kinney & Munroe, 2001). In Olympia, Washington, middle school students tutor student teachers from a local college in how to use high-tech tools (Armstrong, 2001). In each of these cases, young teens are being empowered at an age when their biological imperative is demanding that they be recognized.

Honoring and Respecting Student Voices

A deeper manifestation of giving students significant roles in decision making in the school is the respect that needs to be given to their authentic voices. This may be the most important thing that educators at the middle school level can do for their students: help them find their own true voice. Students at this age are struggling with a myriad of inner voices internalized from peers, gangs, the media, and other sources, and in the midst of all of this, they are faced with the significant challenge of trying to pick from that hodgepodge of noises their own unique identity—their own true voice.

Teachers in middle schools should be greatly concerned with helping students develop their own individual voices through poetry, journal writing, and other meaningful writing assignments. At Broad Meadows Middle School in Quincy, Massachusetts, students engage in a program called Writing Wrongs. Instead of writing phony business letters from a textbook, they write real letters to real people to solve real problems. One letter persuaded a mayor to adopt the student's own adopt-a-neighborhood cleanup program. Other students wrote letters to politicians and businesspeople about child labor practices in third world countries, and as a result they testified before the U.S. Department of Labor, addressed graduate students at Harvard, and raised $147,000 to set up a school in Pakistan for children in bonded labor (Adams, 2001). As young teens notice their deeper voices being listened to and recognized, they acquire confidence and a sense of selfhood that will stand them in good stead as they face the challenges of the future.

Facilitating Social and Emotional Growth

Academic Achievement Discourse puts social and emotional growth on the back burner while it goes about its work of meeting standards and boosting test scores. Yet educators do this at great peril to society. Good middle schools help students develop their emotional intelligence and their intrapersonal and interpersonal intelligence (Gardner, 1993; Goleman, 1997). They use cooperative learning as a key to fostering positive social relationships. They have well-trained counselors on staff and maintain good referral networks for students needing special help with their emotional problems from mental health professionals. They engage students in curriculum-related activities that serve to develop their social and emotional intelligences.

At Webb Middle School in Austin, Texas, students create life graphs or visual autobiographies that depict the ups and downs of their lives, including trips, accidents, family milestones, and other personally meaningful events. They then choose an event from the graph to expand into a written narrative such as "How I Learned to Play Basketball," "A Trip to Mexico," or "Being Made Fun Of." They also create identity boxes that contain photos, relics, poems, and other treasures, and they are then videotaped presenting their boxes to the rest of the class (Appelsies & Fairbanks, 1997). At Walden III Middle School in Racine, Wisconsin, students go through a Rites of Passage Experience that involves presenting evidence of competence in 16 areas, including English, math, ethics, and physical challenge, to a committee of teachers, peers, and community members (George Lucas Educational Foundation, 1997). By giving primary attention to the development of social and emotional learning in middle school, educators ensure that students will have the personal tools they need in order to function optimally in the broader society around them.

Too many educators believe that early adolescence is either a time for whipping kids into shape for the academic rigors of high school or a time for patient (if painful) endurance while they go about their tortuous process of growing up. It is neither. There is a great middle area between these two extremes that must be the focus of those who wish to deal with the reality of young teens. Young adolescents live rich and intense lives. To demand that they leave these lives outside of the school boundaries is to commit a serious injustice to them, and it also threatens to deprive society of the gifts these kids have to give. By embracing the passion of early adolescence and using that energy to revitalize the classroom, educators will ensure that these vibrant young voices will sing out their hopes, fears, joys, and sorrows in a way that can benefit not only themselves but the rest of society as well.

For Further Study

1. Visit a middle school that employs some of the developmentally appropriate practices described in this chapter. Then visit a middle school that follows some of the developmentally inappropriate practices examined in the chapter. Compare your experiences. What was the general emotional tone of each school? Where did students appear to be learning more? Where did they seem most involved in the learning process? Discuss your reflections and observations with colleagues who have visited the same or similar schools.

2. Think back to your own early adolescence. What were some of your hopes, fears, joys, and dreams? What particular problems took center stage at that time in your life? What was school like for you? Do you remember any teachers who were particularly supportive or unsupportive? What courses, activities, and learning experiences do you remember enjoying the most (and the least) in school? Write down your memories as they come to you. Share them with a colleague (or a group of colleagues) who have gone through the same process. Discuss what has changed about being a young teen since you were that age.

3. Observe young teens involved in formal and informal learning activities inside and outside of school. What sorts of inferences can you make about their emotional, social, and creative lives based on the behaviors that you see? How do the environments you observe them in either support or not support their developmental needs?

4. Ask at least five adolescents between the ages of 11 and 15 what they think about school. Ask them what their favorite and least favorite courses are in school. Ask them about their favorite and least favorite teachers (do this in a school where you are *not* one of the teachers). If they don't enjoy their school experience, ask them what sorts of changes might make their time in school more satisfying to them.

5. Which of the developmentally appropriate practices for young adolescents described in this chapter are most important in your opinion? What other practices would you add to this list? Which practices seem most absent from the middle schools in your area? Support the development and implementation of one or more of these practices in your district or community.

6

High Schools: Preparing Students to Live Independently in the Real World

On February 26, 2005, Bill Gates, the founder of Microsoft and one of the richest people on earth, addressed governors, CEOs, and leading educators at the National Education Summit on High Schools held in Washington, D.C. In his address, Gates called the American high school obsolete. He decried the lack of preparedness of most high school graduates for college and work in the 21st century. He recommended that high school be reformed so that all students who graduate will be ready for college. Gates noted in his speech: "We have one of the highest high school dropout rates in the industrialized world. Many who graduate do not go on to college. And many who do go on to college are not well-prepared—and end up dropping out. That is one reason why the U.S. college dropout rate is also one of the highest in the industrialized world" (Gates, 2005). There is a certain irony in Mr. Gates's comments. He was a college dropout.

Gates left Harvard in 1975 to found Microsoft, and the rest, as they say, is history. But that's not the end of the story. The list of billionaire college dropouts is an astonishing one, and includes Paul Allen (Microsoft), Michael Dell (Dell Computers), Larry Ellison (Oracle), Steve Jobs (Apple, Pixar), and Richard Branson (Virgin Records), who skipped college entirely (Dukcevich, 2003). Multi-millionaire food mogul dropouts include Ray Kroc (McDonald's), Colonel Sanders (KFC), Dave Thomas (Wendy's), Fred Delucca (Subway), Tom Monaghan (Domino's Pizza), and Carl Karcher (Carl's Jr.). Other college dropouts or no-shows include the great psychoanalyst Erik Erikson and writer William Faulkner.

Graduating from college, it appears, is *not* a prerequisite for success in life. And yet Bill Gates was at least partially right in his assessment. Our high schools *are* obsolete to the extent that they are not preparing students to live as successful and independent adults in the real world. In this chapter, I am going to suggest that this is the single most important function of high schools. But I am also going to suggest that a four-year academic college is only one option among many for which high schools should prepare their students. Other post–high school possibilities include nontraditional programs in four-year colleges, alternative four-year institutions, two-year community colleges, trade and technical schools, registered apprenticeship programs, skills centers, correspondence and online programs, work-study or travel-study courses, and direct involvement in entrepreneurial activities in the same way that Gates and the other billionaires mentioned above took the world by storm.

Academic Achievement Discourse significantly narrows the focus of how educators think about preparing students for life after graduation. Recent federal legislation proposes to provide college scholarships to students who complete a "rigorous" high school program. It will be up to the federal government to decide exactly what "rigor" means (the *Oxford English Dictionary* defines it as "severity in dealing with a person"). It is likely that such a program will look something like the following: four years of English, three and a half years of social studies, two years of foreign language, and a year each of algebra, geometry, advanced algebra, biology, chemistry, and physics (Dillon, 2006). Even this is not enough in today's Academic Achievement Discourse climate. Now an academic four-year-college climate is being built into the very structure of many high schools. Advanced Placement courses have grown from involving just a few students at top high schools 50 years ago to implementation in more than 60 percent of U.S. high schools today. In his 2006 State of the Union message, President Bush proposed to "train 70,000 high school teachers to lead advanced-placement courses in math and science," which would quadruple the number of students taking AP classes to 1.5 million by 2012 (Lewin, 2006).

Such a path of preparation may be fine for students who are planning to be doctors, lawyers, scientists, or professors. But what about students who have other goals? What about students who plan to be beauticians, plumbers, paralegals, secretaries, child care workers, contractors, or any of hundreds of other professions that don't require a four-year academic college degree? Such intense focus on highly academic college preparation serves only to fuel the frustration of many of these students, whose dreams, abilities, aspirations, and proclivities are not reflected in this drive to treat all students the same, as if they were all supposed to *want* highly academic training in order to succeed in life. And what about students who don't even know what they want to do with their lives? By locking these individuals into a tight academic sequence of courses, we deprive them of the opportunity of trying out other career possibilities while they are still in high school (through internships, apprenticeships, and other programs that will be described later on in this chapter). These kinds of experiences would put them in a far better position to evaluate how they want to prepare for the rest of their lives.

Developmental Needs of Middle and Late Adolescence

This tunnel vision of how high schools are preparing students for their future overlooks many important developmental issues. Students in middle and late adolescence are on the threshold of becoming independent human adults. In ancient and indigenous cultures, after making it through puberty rites, adolescents were considered adults and engaged in adult responsibilities. Such ceremonies are reflected even today in Hispanic culture through the quinceañera—or the flowering of a girl into Latina womanhood at the age of 15—and in the bat mitzvah or bar mitzvah ceremonies of Judaism, when 12-year-old girls become women and 13-year-old boys become men. From a juridical perspective, there is a clear recognition of the growing maturity of the middle teen years. Fourteen-year-olds may legally work in many nonhazardous occupations and set up their own individual retirement accounts. Sixteen-year-olds can legally drive in most states, and in many states they can legally marry under certain conditions. At 18 years of age, adolescents are able to vote in local, state, and federal elections. It's rather ironic to note that in the real world, high school–aged individuals are accorded many adult privileges, but when they are sitting in a high school classroom, they still have to raise their hand if they want to go to the bathroom!

From a biological perspective, kids in the middle and late teen years have made it past the initial shock waves of puberty and are beginning to settle down neurologically. After a spike in the amount of gray matter during the initial stages of puberty, a thinning out or pruning process takes place that allows the brain to work more efficiently. White matter, or the part of the brain that permits nerve impulses to travel more quickly, steadily increases as the individual approaches the age of 20 and beyond. The frontal lobes, where higher cognitive functions take place, are still maturing well into late adolescence and early adulthood (Giedd et al., 1999; Rapoport et al., 1999).

However, many positive developmental changes are taking place during middle adolescence (ages 15 to 17), including the ability to develop coherent plans and long-term goals, the capacity to analyze problems with greater facility, and the capability to ask deeper questions about moral, ethical, and religious issues. Kids at this age have developed a more stable sense of self than younger teens as a result of several new factors, including widening social networks, increasing intellectual awareness of the world, reflection gained from time in solitude, and discovery of new talents and abilities in such areas as sports, art, and music.

Amid all these changes, high schools concerned with preparing students for the future should be aware of the developmental needs not just of adolescence but of the next stage of human development: young adulthood. As it turns out, graduating from a four-year academic institution is not one of the central developmental tasks of young adulthood, according to most human development researchers. Erik Erikson (1993) noted in his acclaimed model of human development that the key issue of young adulthood is the quest for intimacy (failing which the individual remains isolated). Young adulthood is the age when most people marry, have children, and raise their families. It is also the time when most people take on their first real jobs and go through some kind of mentoring as well as a process of trial and error in determining how best to fit their uniqueness into the cultural demands around them (Kenniston, 1972; Levinson, 1986, 1997). There is nothing in the current college prep push in secondary institutions that reflects *any kind of awareness at all* of the need to prepare students for these future developmental tasks. A school that focuses all of its resources on preparing students to pass tests in calculus, physics, and chemistry has little time left to help students reflect on who they are, how to get along with others, how to nurture other living beings, and how to discover inner preferences and proclivities to fuel future career aspirations.

Developmentally Inappropriate Practices at the High School Level

Many of the problems that were discussed in the previous chapter regarding middle schools are also relevant at the high school level, including the damaging effects of large, impersonal schools, unsafe school climates, emotionally flat learning experiences, and fragmented curricula. One of the most significant efforts historically to address many of these issues at the secondary level has come from Theodore Sizer and his Coalition of Essential Schools. Sizer and his colleagues have criticized many features of the traditional comprehensive high school, including the chopping up of the class day into 50-minute segments, the extensive lecturing by teachers *at* students, and the haphazard accumulation of course credits in disparate and irrelevant subject areas—the so-called "shopping mall high school" (Herbst, 1996; Powell, Farrar, & Cohen, 1985; Sizer, 2004). As Sizer put it: "Can anyone at all argue, for example, that an adolescent's intellectual development is best pursued by exposure in 50-minute snippets to sharply differentiated subjects, each planned in total isolation from the others? Can anyone believe that students should be the passive recipients of teacher's talk for up to 90 percent of the time?" (Cushman, 1989, para. 17). Similarly, high school reformer Deborah Meier has criticized the failure of secondary institutions to engage students in genuine dialogue about the world that challenges them to create their own questions, ideas, and solutions to life's problems (Meier, 2002). Along with and related to the previously noted developmentally inappropriate practices are some others that merit discussion (see also Figure 6.1):

Tracking. The process of putting students into different "ability groups" or "tracks" (for example, academic/vocational or college prep/basic/general) significantly lowers the quality of the learning experience for those students who are placed in the bottom or lower tracks. Oakes (2005) noted that teaching in the lower tracks tended to consist of rote learning and memorization, the use of

boring workbooks and kits, and practice in survival skills such
as filling out a job application, while students in the upper tracks
engaged in higher-order problem solving, critical thinking, creative
writing, and other more developmentally appropriate activities.
Making administrative decisions about students' futures before
their brains have fully developed, before the students themselves
have been given a voice in their career aspirations, and from what
are more often social and racial inequities than real differences
between individuals condemns many students to living lives that
do not match their own developmental potential.

Figure 6.1

Developmentally Inappropriate and Appropriate Practices in High School

Developmentally Inappropriate Practices	Developmentally Appropriate Practices
Large, impersonal high schools	Small learning communities
"Shopping mall" high schools	Theme-based magnet or charter schools
Tracking	Career academies
Too much time sitting in classrooms	Internships
Excessive academic pressure	Entrepreneurial enterprises
Impersonal student–teacher relationships	Apprenticeships
Zero-tolerance policies	Democratic communities

Too Much Time Sitting in a Classroom. If the purpose of high
school, as I have articulated it, is to prepare students for independent life in the real world, then the more time students sit at
cramped desks in fluorescent-lit classrooms, the less time they
have to spend engaging in this key developmental task. To some
hardheaded educators, it might appear as if responding to school
bells, getting a pass to use the restroom, listening to unexpected
announcements over the public address system, and pushing
around a No. 2 pencil is a great way to become accustomed to the
ways of the real world. Two things, however, are missing from this
scenario. One is a sense of independence. The other is the real

world. In the real world, people are negotiating, mediating, articu-
lating, arguing, manufacturing, experimenting, planning, reflecting, designing, building, teaching, playing, relating, anticipating,
and creating, among many other endeavors. And they're doing it
without a net beneath them. In other words, they're on their own.
The more the school day consists of highly controlled, artificially
contrived, teacher-directed activities, the more developmentally
inappropriate that school environment will be.

Excessive Academic Pressure. This book has already discussed
the deleterious effects of Academic Achievement Discourse on
students at all levels. Even for students who are themselves highly
motivated and adapted to pursue a strictly academic preparation
for college, the piling on of AP courses, the struggle to get not just
a 4.0 average but something higher, and the striving to meet more
and more rigorous class course loads create stresses that are inimi-
cal to students' deeper developmental needs. These students, like
everyone else at this age, are busy constructing identities, forming
relationships, asking deeper questions about life, and becoming
more independent from parents, teachers, and the past. If their
hours and days are spent in an endless pursuit of the highest grade
point average possible and a 5 on every AP course they can take,
then their identities are going to form around this thin crust of self
and may easily collapse if the stresses become too great or the
structure of life around them changes and they are unable to adapt.
Depression, eating disorders, suicide attempts, and other mental
(and physical) illnesses wait in the wings for adolescents who
have chosen to walk this high wire without having been given any
instruction in the art of life during their time in high school.

The Best Schools: Examples of Developmentally Appropriate Practices in High School

Many developmentally appropriate practices suited for the secondary level have already been covered in the previous chapter

on middle schools. In addition, a number of broad principles have been clearly articulated by the Coalition of Essential Schools. Developed for both elementary and secondary levels (including middle school), these common principles lay out a framework for the kinds of elements that should be present in *all* schools, regardless of the specific programs or curricula used in any particular setting (Sizer, 1997b). They include the following:

- Helping students learn to use their minds well.
- Recognizing that less is more; focusing on depth over coverage.
- Having goals apply to all students.
- Personalizing teaching and learning.
- Practicing a student-as-worker, teacher-as-coach approach.
- Emphasizing demonstration of mastery.
- Communicating a tone of decency and trust.
- Expressing a commitment to the entire school.
- Dedicating resources to teaching and learning.
- Honoring and modeling democracy and equity.

These principles do not reflect specific developmental differences between age groups, but they do represent some of the key features that must be part of a school's inner structure if students' developmental needs are to be met. If I were to inject any kind of developmental component into these principles, it would be a recognition of the changing nature of the student–teacher relationship through the different developmental periods. At the early childhood level, I would view the relationship in terms of *student as player, teacher as facilitator;* at the elementary school level, *student as worker, teacher as coach;* at the middle school level, *student as explorer, teacher as guide;* and at the high school level, *student as apprentice, teacher as mentor.* This last relationship acknowledges the fact that high school students are on the verge of becoming independent young adults and can thrive best in the presence of adults who are "expert adults," both in the sense of modeling mature adult thinking and behavior and in the sense of having specific expertise in particular subjects (mechanics, history, cinema, fiber art, philosophy, etc.) that they can pass on to the next generation.

There are a wide range of specific programs, structures, and curricula at the high school level that are particularly suitable for allowing students to practice the skills of becoming an independent adult. These best practices all share the common element of treating students as emerging adults instead of big kids and recognizing that the best learning environments are those that take place not in an artificially designed educational climate, but in the midst of the ambiguity and complexity of the real world. Career days, field trips, classroom simulations, and guest speakers in school, which were excellent activities at the elementary school level, are no longer sufficient ways of quenching the thirst adolescents have for becoming part of the adult world. Instead, at least some of the following approaches need to be incorporated as key components of any developmentally based high school.

Theme-Based Magnet and Charter Schools. These are schools that have been designed around specific career-related themes that involve actual practice in real-world skills. One example is Aviation High School in Long Island City, New York. It is the only school in the country that features a hangar with small aircraft. Students work in conventional classrooms as well as professionally run shops to test, fabricate, and fix airplane parts. High school graduates earn a Federal Aviation Administration certificate either in air frame (the plane's body) or power plant (its engine). At West Hawaii Explorations Academy, Hawaii's first charter school, students engage in ecological studies as a focus. Situated on the grounds of the Natural Energy Lab on the lava-covered Kona coast, students engage in projects covering alternative energy development, research in sustainability of the environment, and aquaculture. Students may develop hypotheses for restoring brackish ponds, design and build energy-efficient vehicles, or use computerized probes to measure oxygen and heat out in the field (Curtis, 2001b). In Brooklyn, New York, students learn firefighting and safety skills at the FDNY High School for Fire and Life Safety. Students spend time with former firefighters, practice emergency scenarios, and have the opportunity to become emergency medical technicians, to become firefighters (with some college credit hours and a certification exam), or to pursue training in related fields such as the health industry, photography, or building inspection (Zehr, 2005).

Career Academies. These are usually schools within schools that permit a group of 100–150 students to stay with a core group of teachers throughout their high school experience (Kemple & Scott-Clayton, 2004). Academic courses are integrated with technical and applied courses organized around a career theme. The academy works in conjunction with community businesses that provide financial and technical support. The first career academy was the Electrical Academy at Edison High School in Philadelphia, started in 1969 and sponsored by Philadelphia Electric Company. Other career academies have focused on a wide range of subjects including automotive studies, environmental technology, law, horticulture, computers, tourism, and health. At Oakland Technical High School, around 175 students participate in the Oakland Health and Bioscience Academy. Sophomores are matched with career mentors and do 100 hours of community service in local hospitals. Juniors rotate through a series of after-school careers, and by their senior year many students are earning wages or school credit, or both, by engaging in after-school internships. The classes of most career academies meet the requirements for entering four-year colleges and universities.

Internships. This alternative permits high school students to work onsite with organizations and businesses for a period of time to learn about a particular industry or occupation. Students' workplace activities may involve a sample of tasks from different jobs, or several tasks from a single occupation. Internships may occur as part of the school week, as an after-school component, or during the summertime. They may be volunteer positions or include financial compensation. Internships may be arranged through the school, with an internship placement organization, or through the companies or organizations themselves. For example, educators at Lakeside High School in northern Idaho have developed internships for the six career pathways at their school: business and marketing, human and social services, science and engineering, production and industrial, arts and communications, and natural resources. Students engaged in the natural resources internship program learn how to locate, inspect, and clean nesting sites for Canada geese, wood ducks, and bluebirds, and meet with botanists, conservationists, and other specialists to learn about their occupations and also about how to prepare for employment with the U.S. Forest Service (Foemmel, 1997).

Entrepreneurial Enterprises. These programs provide opportunities for high school students to design and operate a business inside or outside of the classroom. A computer teacher and five students in McDermott, Nevada, could not find an affordable Internet service provider (ISP) for their school computer network, so they formed their own nonprofit ISP company, which not only serviced the school's 72 computers but also provided online service to 165 residents and businesses in the surrounding area (Trotter, 2000). Students in Ouray, Colorado, operate KURA-LP 98.9 FM, one of only a few radio stations managed and produced by high school students 24 hours a day, seven days a week, all year long. Students at Salem High School in Massachusetts operate their own bistro in the basement called the Black Cat Café (Wade, 2004). A number of national organizations exist to support students in learning about the logistics of the business world and in creating their own businesses, including Junior Achievement, Future Business Leaders of America, Distributive Education Clubs of America, and Future Farmers of America.

Apprenticeships. These are school-to-work experiences in specific occupational areas designed to lead directly to a related post secondary program, an entry-level job, or a registered apprenticeship program. Registered apprenticeship programs are relationships in which the worker, or apprentice, learns an occupation from an employer or employee in a structured program sponsored by employers or labor unions. At the Fox Cities Apprenticeship Program in Appleton, Wisconsin, for example, juniors and seniors learn the printing trade by attending Fox Valley Technical School two days a week and participating in workplace learning during the other three days. Students spend a year rotating through a printing company, observing various aspects of the operations before assuming their own work-related roles.

Service Learning. These programs provide students with volunteer positions in nonprofit community organizations that serve to help the environment, young children, elders, the sick, the poor, or others in need. They also give students an opportunity to reflect on their experiences in a school setting and link service learning with academic learning. In the state of Maryland, for example, where service to the community has been made a requirement for high school graduation, students clean out horse stalls, answer telephone hotlines, ladle soup for the homeless, and build houses for the organization Habitat for Humanity. These activities, in turn, lead to new interests, aspirations, and questions about housing, poverty, ecology, and other important social issues (Galley, 2003).

Mentoring. These types of programs match a student with an adult (in or outside the school) who has the skills and knowledge desired to be mastered by the student. The mentor instructs, critiques, coaches, and challenges the student to do well, working in cooperation with the school or the student's employer. At Met West, in Oakland, California, for example, a veterinary technician mentors a student as she gives vaccines, cleans cages, trims nails, and cares for the animals at Broadway Pet Hospital in downtown Oakland (Furger, 2004b). At Berkeley Vale Community High School in Australia, students are paired with retired and semiretired individuals in the community for mentor relationships of up to one year. Student and mentor meet once a week and keep in touch by telephone during the week to research occupations, visit workplaces, and make inquiries. The mentor keeps a record of the career development of the young person and looks out for opportunities and contacts.

Cooperative Education. Originally implemented in Cincinnati, Ohio, in 1906, cooperative education has evolved into programs that either tend to alternate a semester of classroom learning with a semester of paid employment or that split the day into a morning spent in the classroom and an afternoon spent in the workplace (Kerka, 1999). A written evaluation plan structures the student's co-op experience in conjunction with school and workplace authorities.

Job Shadowing. In this scenario, a student follows an employee at a place of business to learn about a particular occupation or industry. These experiences can range from one-time-only visits of a few hours to periodic visits over a longer period of time. One study of students who participated in a Junior Achievement job shadowing program reported that their experiences helped them develop a better understanding of the relationship between education and getting a good job, the complexities of the business world, and what it takes to be successful in the workplace (Van Dusen & Edmundson, 2003).

Educational Release. These programs provide students with a leave of absence from school to engage in real-world pursuits, including foreign travel, foreign exchange programs, missionary work, studies in other locations, or workplace experiences, to improve employability status or personal development. It is rather interesting to note that prestigious colleges like Harvard, Cornell, and Sarah Lawrence often recommend that accepted applicants take a year off (typically called a "gap year") to travel or work before they start their freshman year (Pope, 2005).

The programs listed above are only some of the many opportunities for high school students to engage in real-world activities while getting high school (and sometimes college) credit and employment skills. Proponents of Academic Achievement Discourse may wonder how students who are intent on an academic vocation requiring significant higher education, such as the law, medicine, academia, or research science, could possibly benefit from (or find time for) these programs, many of which have been associated in times past with the "low-performing students" (an Academic Achievement Discourse phrase) in a school. The truth is that many students may not even know if they want to go into the legal, medical, scientific, or academic profession unless and until they have had the opportunity to intern with, job shadow, or be mentored by lawyers, doctors, scientists, or college professors. The presence of such programs in our nation's high schools will help ensure that students have some sense of where they are going before they decide on the kind of postsecondary education or workplace training they w ill pursue. At the same time, by viewing the high school experience primarily in terms of preparing students for real-life roles, students who feel disenfranchised, bored, or alienated in academic classes that have little or no relationship to their particular needs or interests will have the opportunity to discover their own unique paths to success in adulthood.

For Further Study

1. Look up archived news information concerning one or more nationally covered incidents of high school violence that have occurred in the past 10 years. As you discover more about the perpetrators of the violence, note what kind of high schools they attended, what sorts of classes they took, and what kinds of relationships they had with peers, teachers, and administrators. Were the high schools oriented more toward academic achievement or human development? What reflections do you have on how high schools should be reformed based on your investigations of these schools?

2. Interview two or three high school students about their experiences in high school. What courses do they like and dislike? How concerned are they about grades and test scores? What kinds of plans do they have for postsecondary work or study? Where do they see themselves in five years? In 10 years? What sorts of reflections can you make about their high school experience based

on your interviews? Can you make any inferences about the high school experience in general from these interviews?

3. Recall your own experiences in high school. What sorts of plans did you have for the future? What kinds of preparations did you make in high school based on those plans? Did you have encouragement or support from teachers, administrators, counselors, or other high school personnel to pursue your plans? How did your plans for the future actually match up with the realities of your adult life? Do you feel that your high school did a good job of preparing you to live independently in the real world? Why or why not? What inferences can you make from your own high school experiences to the kind of high schools that kids in today's world need?

4. Investigate some of the developmentally appropriate practices described in this chapter by visiting one or more high schools in your area. Are there certain high schools that have more of a Human Development Discourse focus and others that are oriented more toward Academic Achievement Discourse? What factors have made certain high schools more inclined toward academic achievement and others toward human development?

5. Design your ideal developmental high school. What sorts of programs, courses, and activities would go on there? What kinds of alliances would there be with community, state, national, and international organizations and businesses? How do you envisage teacher roles in such a school? What would it take to begin implementing such a program in your community?

Conclusion

Readers who have followed my arguments to the end of this book undoubtedly have questions about many of the points that I've made. This is understandable, given the fact that I have challenged many entrenched beliefs about how schools should be structured. I'd like to anticipate some of these questions and provide some appropriate responses.

One question on the minds of educators may be phrased something like this: "You've described many terrific practices in the schools you cite, but can you assure me that these schools have also improved their scores on standardized tests?" I'm afraid that I'm going to disappoint many of you with my answer, which is: "I haven't checked, and I'm not particularly interested in finding out." It's entirely possible that they have, but the reason I'm not terribly concerned is that I suspect this question is just a devious way to get me to start talking the language of Academic Achievement Discourse. Yes, I could have followed the first six chapters with a final chapter saying: "Just in case some of you are feeling nervous about what I've said thus far in the book, here are some statistical results showing that you can promote children's growth and development and *still* raise test scores and maintain adequate yearly progress." I did not write such a chapter because it would have sent a message that human development goals in education are important *only if* they promote academic achievement. This would have plunged me into the language of Academic Achievement Discourse.

The point I am making in this book is that we've had too much practice speaking this discourse; we need to try speaking a different language—the language of human development—for a refreshing change. True, there are educators working in the field who have done an excellent job of integrating human development issues with academic achievement goals (see, for example, Comer, 2004). And yes, I believe that ultimately there needs to be a kind of rapprochement between these two different discourses. But one cannot attain such a rapprochement or synthesis until both discourses have been fully explored in the marketplace of ideas. It is clear to me that Academic Achievement Discourse has so overwhelmed the conversation in education with its gargantuan voice that Human Development Discourse can barely be heard. If we were to stop speaking the language of Academic Achievement Discourse entirely for a few years and carry on our discourse in education solely through the voices of human development thinkers, I suspect that only then would there begin to be a kind of parity between these two discourses.

A second question that deserves mentioning goes something like this: "Dr. Armstrong, what you say about human development and the types of practices you recommend are very well and good for students who are already achieving well academically. But what about those students—the majority of them poor and minority kids—who are far behind in academic achievement? In order for them to catch up and have an equal chance of competing in the real world for well-paying jobs, won't all this focus on human development and this neglect of academic achievement and test scores do them a great disservice?" This is the "closing the achievement gap" question. It has been this argument that has driven much of the government rhetoric in the past four decades and helped influence the passage of the No Child Left Behind Act. This is the argument that has given Academic Achievement Discourse much of its legal force and moral justification. However, there are significant flaws in this argument. First of all, the gap mentioned above is generally defined in terms of test score results, and the implication is that all we have to do is raise the test scores of poorly achieving students to the level of achieving students and we will have accomplished our goal. This is what "closing the gap" actually means in literal terms. However, this is a superficial response to a very deep and complex set of problems that relate to social, racial, and economic inequities that exist at the very core of our social system. The gap that really exists in education has been very well articulated by Jonathan Kozol (1992, 2005), who strongly argues that schools in poor and minority areas do not have the budgets, materials, resources, training, or infrastructure to equal those schools in wealthy districts that happen to have the highest test results in the country. Consequently, they are in no position to compete with those schools, academically or otherwise.

This is a question of equity, not test results. Poor and minority students deserve to have the same high-quality learning experiences described in this book as rich white kids. They don't deserve to have developmentally inappropriate practices such as test preparation kits and boring textbooks thrust upon them just because politicians believe they need to close the achievement gap, and yet Kozol suggests that they are far more likely to get this kind of treatment. Such efforts to close "the achievement gap" may actually end up proving counterproductive. Recent negotiated changes in the No Child Left Behind Act, for example, have been seen to benefit whites more than minorities (Sunderman, 2006).

I'd also like to look at the "show me the money" question, which I believe is the soundest argument to challenge the perspective I've taken in this book. This question goes something like this: "You say we need to take academic achievement less seriously than we have in the past. Yet there are some hard statistics out there showing that the more academic education students get after high school, the more money they are going to make during their lifetime. Won't your eschewing academic achievement in favor of human development serve to deprive many students of potentially hundreds of thousands of dollars in lost income as a result of not going on in school?" First, let me point out that I am *not* saying that students should not pursue education after high school. I am well aware of the statistics that show the correlation between higher education and yearly income (U.S. Census Bureau, 2002). I am completely and absolutely in favor of students graduating from high school and going on to get whatever education or training they need in order to accomplish their personal and professional goals.

The problem is that by creating an environment during the first 12 years of schooling that focuses on education not as a means of personal fulfillment but as a way of obtaining high test scores, we condemn many kids to school frustration and subsequent abandonment of school altogether. If students drop out of high school because the curriculum is neither meeting their personal needs for development nor recognizing their need to grow as unique human beings, then they are going to end up at the bottom of the income ladder for the rest of their lives. Similarly, if we prepare students for higher education by emphasizing their performance on test scores and neglect to help them understand their potentials and aspirations, then many students who go on to college will likewise feel disenfranchised and drop out before the completion of a degree. Human Development Discourse is concerned with helping students understand their *own* development (where they have been, where they are now, where they are going in life) so that the decisions they make about higher education and career choices will be congruent with their inner needs. If we follow the logic of the "show me the money" argument, then educators ought to encourage *all* students to go to professional schools (medical school, law school, etc.) because the statistics show that this level of education is associated with the highest income. We don't make that demand (or at least most of us don't) because we realize that people are different and have different aspirations, different needs, different interests, and different capacities. Thank goodness for the diversity, or our society would be made up solely of doctors and lawyers! Yes, money is good, money is important, but there are other things out there called values—honesty, integrity, courage, trust, altruism, beauty, cooperation, empathy, hope—that are qualities that ultimately make life worth living and that deserve to be considered as the most important goals of the educational process.

In conclusion, I want to reflect on the state of contemporary culture and its relationship to education. It doesn't take a social scientist to understand that our society and the wider world are plagued with social ills: poverty, injustice, violence, starvation, prejudice, war, disease. You name it; we're dealing with it. We're also passing them along to the next generation. How do we best equip our kids to deal with these problems? By worrying them to death about how they're going to do on next week's test? By threatening that they won't graduate if they don't muscle under and memorize the periodic table of elements? By taking away their favorite activity if they don't keep their grade point average up? By taking them out of the sandbox at age 3 and plunking them down at a computer station? These are only a few of the burdens that Academic Achievement Discourse has placed on those very students that we are counting on to create a peaceful, plentiful, and equitable society in the future.

As I've pointed out elsewhere (Armstrong, 1998), the true survival skills in education are the ones we provide our students that will enable humanity to continue to evolve as a species. Academic Achievement Discourse is not up to the challenge of providing these life-preserving skills to the next generation. Only by standing back from this narrow view and seeing our students in terms of their whole development (past, present, and future) and viewing our own task as educators in terms of supporting that development will we have a good chance of saving this planet and transforming it into a place that is safe for human beings and other living things.

Appendix

**Summary of How Human Development Research
Should Inform Educational Practice**

Summary of How Human Development Research Should Inform Educational Practice

School Level	Ages	Best Educational Setting	Key Focus	Brain Basis	Cultural Antecedents	Curriculum Emphasis	Most Developmentally Appropriate Assessment Approaches	Student–Teacher Relationship
Early Childhood	3–6	Play space	Play	Rich dendritic connections, effect of environmental stimulation on synaptic development	Child not morally responsible until 7	Rich sensorimotor experiences, open-ended imaginative play	Observation and documentation of spontaneous play experiences	Student as player, teacher as facilitator
Elementary School	7–10	Children's museum	Learning how the world works	Cultural pruning of synaptic growth	Formal skill training	Learning about symbol systems, customs, rules, institutions, the natural world	Performance-based assessments of project-based learning (criterion-based, ipsative measures)	Student as worker/learner, teacher as coach
Middle School/Junior High	11–14	Therapeutic milieu	Social, emotional, and metacognitive learning	Limbic system maturity, lack of frontal lobe maturity	Rites of passage (puberty) ceremonies	Affective education, emotional intelligence development, small-group work	Self-assessment (journals, projects), student–teacher review of work, peer review	Student as explorer, teacher as guide
High School	15–18	Apprenticeships	Preparing to live independently in the real world	Progressive development of frontal lobes	Taking on adult roles and responsibilities	Career preparation and development	Portfolios, certification tests, college prep exams	Student as apprentice, teacher as mentor

School Level	Ages	Key Obstacles to Realization	Results of Failure to Employ Appropriate Education Model	Pedagogical Tools	Examples of Actual School Programs	Examples of Misuse of Developmental Goal	Examples of How a Subject Should Be Taught (e.g., Reading)
Early Childhood	3–6	Pushing back developmental timetables, inappropriate use of academic achievement model, demise of play, rise of technologies	Hurried child syndrome, stress symptoms (affecting learning, attention, concentration)	Play house, playground, hands-on sensory-exploration, dress-up, drama, blocks	Roseville Community Preschool, Roseville, CA	Laissez-faire, unsupervised play environments	Not taught at all; only exposure to words, books, etc., as part of the play space
Elementary School	7–10	Focus on standardized testing, paper-and-pencil learning	Learning disabilities, attention deficit disorder, school discipline problems	Activity centers, field trips, theme-based instruction, project-based learning, simulations	Lowell City School MicroSociety, Lowell, MA	Unstructured, activity-based program with few outcomes	Rich literature-based, language-based literacy program (with phonemic awareness as an integral part)
Middle School/ Junior High	11–14	Pressure for academic college preparation and achievement	Gangs, school violence, school apathy, drug use	Active learning, community of learners, affective/social learning, metacognitive strategies	Clarkson School of Discovery, NC	For-profit total milieu therapeutic programs using coercion	Reading for self-discovery, peer reading groups, metacognitive reading strategies
High School	15–18	Pressure for academic four-year college preparation	Gangs, school violence, school apathy, drug use	Apprenticeships, internships, cooperative education, career counseling	Aviation High School, Long Island, NY	Unsupervised work experiences	Reading for pleasure, work roles, and college preparation

References

Adams, R. (2001, August). Writing wrongs, business letters give students a voice in world affairs. *Middle Ground, 5*(1), 36–37.

Alexander, W. M. (1995, January). The junior high school: A changing view. *Middle School Journal, 26*(3), 20–24.

Alliance for Childhood. (2000). *Fool's gold: A critical look at computers in childhood.* College Park, MD: Author. Available: www.allianceforchild hood.net/projects/computers/computers_reports.htm

Almon, J. (2004). Educating for creative thinking: The Waldorf approach. [Online article]. Available: www.waldorfearlychildhood.org/article. asp?id=8

Ambrosio, A. (2003, Fall). Unacceptable: My school and my students are labeled as failures. *Rethinking Schools Online, 18*(1). Available: www. rethinkingschools.org

American Institutes for Research. (2005). *CSRQ Center report on elementary school comprehensive school reform models.* Washington, DC: The Comprehensive School Reform Quality Center.

Anderman, L. H., & Midgley, C. (1998). *Motivation and middle school students.* (Report No. EDO-PS-98-5). Champaign, IL: ERIC Clearinghouse on Elementary and Early Childhood Education. (ERIC Document Reproduction Service No. ED4211281)

Appelsies, A., & Fairbanks, C. M. (1997, May). Write for your life. *Educational Leadership, 54*(8), 70–72.

Archer, J. (2005, August 31). Connecticut files court challenge to NCLB. *Education Week, 25*(1), 23, 27.

Aristotle. (1958). *The pocket Aristotle* (J. D. Kaplan, Ed.). New York: Simon & Schuster.

Armstrong, S. (2001, September 1). Turning the tables—Students teach teachers. *Edutopia Online.* Available: www.edutopia.org/php/article. php?id=Art_797

Armstrong, T. (1988, August). Lessons in wonder. *Parenting,* 44–46.

Armstrong, T. (1990, March). But does it compute? *Parenting,* 27–29.

Armstrong, T. (1991). *Awakening your child's natural genius.* New York: Tarcher/Putnam.

Armstrong, T. (1997). *The myth of the A.D.D. child: 50 ways to improve your child's behavior and attention span without drugs, labels, or coercion.* New York: Plume.

Armstrong, T. (1998). *Awakening genius in the classroom.* Alexandria, VA: Association for Supervision and Curriculum Development.

Armstrong, T. (2000a). *In their own way: Discovering and encouraging your child's multiple intelligences* (Rev. & updated). New York: Penguin/Tarcher.

Armstrong, T. (2000b). *Multiple intelligences in the classroom* (2nd ed.). Alexandria, VA: Association for Supervision and Curriculum Development.

Armstrong, T. (2003a). *ADD/ADHD alternatives in the classroom.* Alexandria, VA: Association for Supervision and Curriculum Development.

Armstrong, T. (2003b). Attention deficit hyperactivity disorder in children: One consequence of the rise of technologies and demise of play? In S. Olfman (Ed.), *All work and no play: How educational reforms are harming our preschoolers* (pp. 161–176). Westport, CT: Praeger.

Armstrong, T. (2005). Canaries in the coal mine: The symptoms of children labeled "ADHD" as biocultural feedback. In G. Lloyd (Ed.), *Critical new perspectives on attention deficit/hyperactivity disorder* (pp. 34–44). London: Routledge.

Association of California School Administrators. (2003, June 9). No Child Left Behind: Middle-grade leaders take a stand on NCLB. *ACSA Online.* Available: www.acsa.org

Association of Children's Museums. (2003, May 2). Whether with public schools, childcare providers or transit authorities, children's museums partner creatively with their communities [Online news release]. Available: www.childrensmuseums.org

Auden, W. H., & Pearson, N. H. (Eds.). (1977). *The portable romantic poets.* New York: Penguin.

Ball, A. (2003, June 2). Geo-literacy: Forging new ground. *Edutopia Online.* Available: www.edutopia.org/php/article.php?id=Art_1042

Ball, A. (2004, December 15). Swamped: Louisiana students become wetlands custodians. *Edutopia Online*. Available: www.edutopia.org/php/article.php?id=Art_1028

Baron-Cohen, S. (1996, June). Is there a normal phase of synaesthesia in development? *Psyche, 2*(27). Available: http://psyche.cs.monash.edu.au/v2/psyche-2-27-baron_cohen.html

Bartlett, J. (1919). *Familiar Quotations, 10th edition*. Boston: Little, Brown.

Bergman, I. (1988). *The magic lantern*. New York: Penguin.

Berliner, D. C. (1993). The 100-year journey of educational psychology: From interest, to disdain, to respect for practice. In T. K. Fagan & G. R. VandenBos (Eds.), *Exploring applied psychology: Origins and critical analyses* (pp. 41–48). (Master Lectures in Psychology). Washington, DC: American Psychological Association.

Bettelheim, B. (1989). *The uses of enchantment: The meaning and importance of fairy tales*. New York: Vintage.

Bishop, P. A., & Pflaum, S. W. (2005, March). Student perceptions of action, relevance, and pace. *Middle School Journal, 36*(4), 4–12. Available: www.nmsa.org/Publications/MiddleSchoolJournal/March2005/Article1/tabid/124/Default.aspx

Blumenfeld, P. C., Soloway, E., Marx, R., Krajcik, J. S., Guzdial, M., & Palincsar, A. (1991). Motivating project-based learning: Sustaining the doing, supporting the learning. *Educational Psychologist, 26*(3 & 4), 369–398.

Blythe, T., White, N., & Gardner, H. (1995). *Teaching practical intelligence: What research tells us*. West Lafayette, IL: Kappa Delta Pi.

Bogdan, R. C., & Bicklen, S. K. (1998). *Qualitative research for education: An introduction to theory and methods* (3rd ed.). Boston: Allyn and Bacon.

Born, L., Shea, A., & Steiner, M. (2002). The roots of depression in adolescent girls: Is menarche the key? *Current Psychiatry Reports, 4*, 449–460.

Bos, B., & Chapman, J. (2005). *Tumbling over the edge: A rant for children's play*. Roseville, CA: Turn the Page Press.

Brandt, R. (1993, April). On teaching for understanding: A conversation with Howard Gardner. *Educational Leadership, 50*(7), 4–7.

Brewster, D. (2005). *Memoirs of the life, writings, and discoveries of Isaac Newton*. Boston: Elibron Classics.

Bruccoli, M. J., & Layman, R. (1994). 1950's education: Overview. *American Decades*. Retrieved July 6, 2006, from http://history.enotes.com/1950-education-american-decades/overview

Bruner, J. (2004). *Toward a theory of instruction*. Cambridge, MA: Belknap Press.

Burbank Elementary School (Hampton, Virginia). (n.d.). Kindergarten homework [Web page]. Retrieved December 12, 2005, from http://bur.sbo.hampton.k12.va.us/pages/KindergartenWebpage/Homework/Homework.html

Carr, S. (2003, September 28). Growing pains: Public Montessori schools still learning [Online article]. *JSOnline: Milwaukee Journal Sentinel,* Available: www.jsonline.com/story/index.aspx?id=173186

Carr, S. (2004, April 4). Blocks, nap time giving way to language and reading programs [Online article]. *JSOnline: Milwaukee Journal Sentinel.* Available: www.jsonline.com/story/index.aspx?id=219303

Casals, P. (1981). *Joys and sorrows: His own story. Pablo Casals as told to Robert E. Kahn.* London: Eel Pie Publishing.

CBS News. (2004, August 25). The "Texas miracle." *60 minutes II,* New York: CBS. Available: www.cbsnews.com/stories/2004/01/06/60II/main591676.shtml

Center on Education Policy. (2005, June). *NCLB: Middle schools are increasingly targeted for improvement.* Washington, DC: Author.

Chugani, H. T. (1998, November). Critical importance of emotional development: Biological basis of emotions: Brain systems and brain development. *Pediatrics, 102*(5), 1225–1229.

Chukovsky, K. (1963). *From two to five.* Berkeley, CA: University of California Press.

Civil Rights Project at Harvard University, The. (2000). *Opportunities suspended: The devastating consequences of zero tolerance and school discipline policies.* Cambridge, MA: The Civil Rights Project at Harvard.

CNN. (1999, August 20). Study: Bullying rampant in U.S. middle schools [Online article]. Available: www.cnn.com/US/9908/20/bullies/index.html

Cole, K. C. (1988, November 30). Play, by definition, suspends the rules. *The New York Times,* p. C16.

Coles, G. (2003, Summer). Learning to read and the "W principle" [Online article]. *Rethinking Schools Online, 17*(4). Available: www.rethinkingschools.org/special-reports/bushplan/wpri174.shtml

Coles, R. (1991). *The spiritual life of children.* New York: Marriner

Coles, R. (2000). *The moral life of children.* New York: Atlantic Monthly Press.

Coles, R. (2003). *Children of crisis.* Boston: Back Bay Books.

Colt, S. (2005, September). Do scripted lessons work—or not? [Online article]. Chevy Chase, MD: Hedrick Smith Productions. Available: www.pbs.org/makingschoolswork/sbs/sfa/lessons.html

Comer, J. (2004). *Leave no child behind: Preparing today's youth for tomorrow's world.* New Haven, CT: Yale University Press.

Comte, A. (1988). *Introduction to positive philosophy* (F. Ferré, Ed. & Rev. Trans.). Indianapolis, IN: Hackett. (Original work published in 1830–42)

Cotton, K. (2001, December). *New small learning communities: Findings from recent literature.* Portland, OR: NWREL.

Csikszentmihalyi, M. (2000, April 19). Education for the 21st century. *Education Week, 19*(32), 46–64.

Cuffaro, H. K. (1984). Microcomputers in education: Why is earlier better? *Teachers College Record, 85,* 559–568.

Currie, J., & Thomas, D. (1995, June). Does Head Start make a difference? *American Economic Review, 85*(3), 341–364.

Curtis, D. (2001a, February 22). We're here to raise kids [Online article]. *Edutopia Online.* Available: www.edutopia.org/php/article. php?id=Art_666

Curtis, D. (2001b, November 1). Classrooms without boundaries [Online article]. *Edutopia Online.* Available: www.edutopia.org/php/article. php?id=Art_885

Cushman, K. (1989, November). At the five-year mark: The challenge of being "Essential" [Online article]. *Horace, 6*(1). Available: www. essentialschools.org/cs/resources/view/ces_res/76

Delisio, E. R. (2001, July 17). How do you spell "stress relief"? [Online article]. *Education World.* Available: www.educationworld.com/a_issues/ issues/issues181.shtml

Denzin, N., & Lincoln, Y. (Eds.). (2005). *The Sage book of qualitative research* (3rd ed.). Thousand Oaks, CA: Sage.

DeVoe, J. F., Peter, K., Kaufman, P., Ruddy, S., Miller, A., Planty, M., et al. (2002, November). *Indicators of school crime and safety: 2002.* Washington, DC: U.S. Departments of Education and Justice.

Dewey, J. (1897, January). My pedagogic creed. *School Journal, 54,* 77–80.

Diamond, M., & Hopson, J. (1998). *Magic trees of the mind: How to nurture your child's intelligence, creativity, and healthy emotions from birth through adolescence.* New York: Dutton.

Dickens, C. (1981). *Hard times.* New York: Bantam.

Dickinson, B. (2001, October 26). Partnership helps local students MUSCLE into math. *Duke* [University] *Dialogue,* p. 12.

Dillon, S. (2006, January 22). College aid plan widens U.S. role in high schools. *The New York Times,* p. 1.

Doda, N. M. (2002). A small miracle in the early years: The Lincoln Middle School story. In N. M. Doda & S. C. Thompson (Eds.), *Transforming ourselves, transforming schools: Middle school change* (pp. 21–42). Westerville, OH: National Middle School Association.

Duckworth, E. (1979, August). Either we're too early and they can't learn it or we're too late and they know it already: The dilemma of applying Piaget. *Harvard Educational Review, 49*(3), 297–312.

Dukcevich, D. (2003, July 28). College vs. no college [Online article]. *Forbes.com.* Available: www.forbes.com/2003/07/28/cx_dd_0728 mondaymatch.html

Edwards, C., Gandini, L., & Foreman, G. (1998). *The hundred languages of children: The Reggio Emilia approach—Advanced reflections.* Greenwich, CT: Ablex.

Eliade, M. (1994). *Rites and symbols of initiation: The mysteries of birth and rebirth*. Dallas, TX: Spring.

Elkind, D. (1987). *Miseducation: Preschoolers at risk*. New York: Knopf.

Elkind, D. (1997). *All grown up and no place to go: Teenagers in crisis*. New York: Perseus.

Elkind, D. (2001a). *The hurried child* (3rd ed.). New York: Perseus.

Elkind, D. (2001b, Summer). Much too early. *Education Next, 1*(2), 9–15.

Engelmann, S. (1981). *Give your child a superior mind: A program for the preschool child*. New York: Cornerstone Library.

Engelmann, S., Haddox, P., & Bruner, E. (1983). *Teach your child to read in 100 easy lessons*. Old Tappan, NJ: Fireside.

Epicurus. (1994). *The Epicurus reader: Selected writings and testimonia* (B. Inwood & L. P. Gerson, Eds. & Trans.). Indianapolis, IN: Hackett.

Erikson, E. H. (1935). Psychoanalysis and the future of education. *Psychoanalytic Quarterly, 4*, 50–68.

Erikson, E. H. (1993). *Childhood and society*. New York: W. W. Norton.

FairTest. (2004). *Fact Sheet: "No Child Left Behind" after three years: An ongoing track record of failure*. Cambridge, MA: Author.

Feller, B. (2005, August 28). In today's kindergarten, more students in for a full day. Associated Press Wire Release.

Finser, T. (1994). *School as a journey*. Hudson, NY: Anthroposophic Press.

Flavell, J. (1963). *The developmental psychology of Jean Piaget*. San Francisco: Van Nostrand Reinholt/John Wiley.

Flesch, R. (1986). *Why Johnny can't read: And what you can do about it*. New York: Harper.

Foemmel, E. (1997). *Natural resource management internship*. NW National Service Symposium, NWREL, Portland, OR.

Freud, S. (2000). *Three essays on the theory of sexuality* (J. Strachey, Trans. & Rev.). New York: Basic Books. (Original work published in 1905)

Froebel, F. (1887). *The education of man*. New York: Appleton & Co.

Furger, R. (2001, August 1). The new P.E. curriculum [Online article]. *Edutopia Online*. Available: www.edutopia.org/php/article.php?id=Art_838

Furger, R. (2004a, March 11). The edible schoolyard [Online article]. *Edutopia Online*. Available: www.edutopia.org/php/article.php?id=Art_1131

Furger, R. (2004b, November/December). High school's new face [Online article]. *Edutopia Online*. Available: www.edutopia.org/magazine/ed1article.php?id=Art_1197&issue=nov_04

Furlow, B. (2001, June 9). Play's the thing. *New Scientist, 170*(2294), 28–31.

Galileo, G. (2001). *Dialogue concerning the two chief world systems* (S. Drake, Trans.). New York: Modern Library. (Original work published in 1632)

Galley, M. (2003, October 15). Md. Service Learning: Classroom link weak? *Education Week, 23*(7), 6.

Gambill, J. (2005). *Interesting insects: 2nd grade.* Paper presented at the Core Knowledge National Conference, Philadelphia, PA. Available: www.coreknowledge.org/CK/resrcs/lessons/05_2_InterestInsects.pdf

Gao, H. (2005, April 11). Kindergarten or "kindergrind"? School getting tougher for kids. *San Diego Union Tribune.*

Gardner, H. (1991). *Art education and human development.* Los Angeles: Getty Trust Publications.

Gardner, H. (1993). *Frames of mind: The theory of multiple intelligences.* New York: Basic Books.

Gardner, H. (1994). Reinventing our schools: A conversation with Dr. Howard Gardner. [Video]. Bloomington, IN: AIT.

Gates, B. (2005, February 26). *Prepared remarks by Bill Gates, co-chair, National Education Summit on High Schools.* Seattle, WA: Bill and Melinda Gates Foundation. Available: www.gatesfoundation.org/MediaCenter/Speeches/BillgSpeeches/BGSpeechNGA-050226.htm

George Lucas Educational Foundation. (1997, July 1). Right of passage. *Edutopia Online.* Available: www.edutopia.org/php/article.php?id=Art_364

George, R., & Hagemeister, M. (2002). *Russia and the czars: Grade 5.* Core Knowledge Conference, Nashville, TN. Available: www.coreknowledge.org/CK/resrcs/lessons/02_5_RussiaandCzars.pdf

Giedd, J. N. (2004). Structural magnetic resonance imaging of the adolescent brain. *Annals of the New York Academy of Sciences, 1021,* 77–85.

Giedd, J. N., Blumenthal, J., Jeffries, N. O., Castellanos, F. X., Liu, H., Zijdenbos, A., et al. (1999, October). Brain development during childhood and adolescence: A longitudinal MRI study. *Nature Neuroscience, 2*(10), 861–863.

Giedd, J. N., Vaituzis, A. C., Hamburger, S. D., Lange, N., Rajapakse, J. C., Kaysen, D., et al. (1996, March). Quantitative MRI of the temporal lobe, amygdala, and hippocampus in normal human development: Ages 4–18 years. *The Journal of Comparative Neurology, 366*(2), 223–230.

Giray, E. F., Altkin, W. M., Vaught, G. M., & Roodin, P. A. (1976, December). The incidence of eidetic imagery as a function of age. *Child Development, 47*(4), 1207–1210.

Glasser, W. (1975). *Schools without failure.* New York: Harper.

Goertzel, V., Goertzel, M., Goertzel, T., & Hansen, A. (2004). *Cradles of eminence: Childhoods of more than 700 famous men and women.* Scottsdale, AZ: Great Potential Press.

Goethe, J. W. von (1989). *The sorrows of young Werther.* New York: Penguin. (Original work published in 1774)

Goldstein, L. F. (2003, April 16). Special education growth spurs cap plan in pending IDEA. *Education Week, 22*(31), 1, 16–17.

Goleman, D. (1997). *Emotional intelligence: Why it can matter more than I.Q.* New York: Bantam.

Goodall, J., & Berman, P. (2000). *Reason for hope: A spiritual journey.* New York: Warner.

Goodman, K. (2005). *What's whole about whole language* (20th anniversary ed.). Muskegon, MI: RDR Books.

Gould, S. J. (1996). *The mismeasure of man.* New York: W. W. Norton.

Halberstam, D. (1993). *The best and the brightest.* New York: Ballantine.

Hansen, L. A. (1998, March/April). Where we play and who we are. *Illinois Parks and Recreation, 29*(2), 22–25.

Harvard Project Zero. (2006). *Active learning practices for schools: Teaching for understanding picture of practice: A year of 8th grade science with Bill McWeeny* [Online resource]. Available: http://learnweb.harvard.edu/alps/tfu/pop3.cfm

Healy, J. M. (1999). *Failure to connect: How computers affect our children's minds—and what we can do about it.* New York: Simon & Schuster.

Henry J. Kaiser Family Foundation. (2004). *Sex education in America.* Menlo Park, CA: Author.

Herbst, J. (1996). *The once and future school: Three hundred and fifty years of American secondary education.* London: Routledge.

Herlihy, C. M., & Kemple, J. J. (2004, December). *The talent development middle school model: Context, components, and initial impacts on students' performance and attendance.* New York: MDRC.

Higgins, L. (2005, January 3). A different way to learn [Online article]. *Detroit Free Press.* Available: www.freep.com/news/education/micro3e_20050103.htm

Hirsch, F. D., Jr. (1988). *Cultural literacy: What every American needs to know.* New York: Vintage.

Hirsch, F. D., Jr. (1999). *The schools we need and why we don't have them.* New York: Anchor.

Hoffman, E. (1994). *The drive for self: Alfred Adler and the founding of individual psychology.* Reading, MA: Addison-Wesley.

Holt, J. (1995). *How children fail.* New York: Perseus.

Huizinga, J. (1986). *Homo ludens.* Boston: Beacon Press.

Husserl, E. (1970). *The crisis of European sciences and transcendental phenomenology.* Evanston, IL: Northwestern University Press.

Illingsworth, R. S., & Illingsworth, C. M. (1969). *Lessons from childhood: Some aspects of the early life of unusual men and women.* London: E. & S. Livingstone.

Jackson, A. W., & Davis, G. A. (2000). *Turning points 2000: Educating adolescents in the 21st century.* New York: Teachers College Press.

Jacobsen, L. (2000, May 10). Huge middle school tries to feel small. *Education Week, 19*(35), 1, 16–17.

Jones, B. F., Rasmussen, C. M., & Moffitt, M. C. (1997). *Real-life problem solving: A collaborative approach to interdisciplinary learning.* Washington, DC: American Psychological Association.

Jung, C. G. (1969). *Psychology and education.* Princeton, NJ: Princeton University Press.

Juvonen, J., Le, V. N., Kaganoff, T., Augustine, C., Constant, L. (2004). *Focus on the wonder years: Challenges facing the American middle school.* Santa Monica, CA: Rand Corp.

Kantrowitz, B., Wingert, P., Brillner, D., Lumsden, M., Grunes, L. D., Kotok, D. (2006, May 8). What makes a high school great. *Newsweek, 47*(10), 50–60.

Karp, S. (2003, November 7). The No Child Left Behind hoax [Online text of talk]. *Rethinking Schools Online.* Available: www.rethinkingschools. org/special_reports/bushplan/hoax.shtml

Kaufmann, W. A. (1988). *Existentialism: From Dostoevsky to Sartre.* New York: Plume.

Kemple, J. J., & Scott-Clayton, J. (2004, March). *Career academies: Impacts on labor market outcomes and educational attainment.* New York: MDRC.

Kenniston, K. (1972). Youth: A new stage of life. In T. J. Cottle (Ed.), *The prospect of youth: Contexts for sociological inquiry* (pp. 631–654). Boston: Little, Brown.

Kerka, S. (1999). *New directions for cooperative education* (ERIC Digest No. 209). Columbus, OH: ERIC Clearinghouse on Adult Career and Vocational Education. (ERIC identifier: ED434245)

Kinney, P., & Munroe, M. (2001). *A school wide approach to student-led conferencing.* Washington, DC: National Middle School Association.

Klein, A. (2006). Public dissatisfied over key NCLB provisions, report says. *Education Week, 25*(34), 8.

Kleiner, C., & Lord, M. (1999, November 22). The cheating game. *U.S. News & World Report, 127*(2), 54.

Klingberg, T., Vaidya, C. J., Gabrieli, J. D., Moseley, M. E., & Hedehus, M. (1999, September 9). Myelination and organization of the frontal white matter in children: A diffusion tensor MRI study. *NeuroReport, 10*(13), 2817–2821.

Knowledge is power. (1957, November 18). *Time, 70*(21), 21–24.

Kohlberg, L. (1981). *The meaning and measurement of moral development.* Worcester, MA: Clark University Heinz Werner Institute.

Kohn, A. (1999). *Punished by rewards: The trouble with gold stars, incentive plans, A's, praise, and other bribes.* Boston: Houghton Mifflin.

Kovalik, S. J. (1993). *ITI, the model: Integrated Thematic Instruction.* Village of Oak Creek, AZ: S. Kovalik & Associates.

Kozloff, M. A., & Bessellieu, F. B. (2000, April). *Direct instruction is developmentally appropriate.* Wilmington, NC: University of North Carolina at

Wilmington. Unpublished paper. Available: http://people.uncw.edu/
kozloffm/didevelapp.html

Kozol, J. (1992). *Savage inequalities: Children in America's schools*. New
York: HarperCollins.

Kozol, J. (2005). *The shame of the nation: The restoration of apartheid
schooling in America*. New York: Crown.

La Mettrie, J. O. (1994). *Man a machine; man a plant* (R. A. Watson &
M. Rybalka, Trans.). Indianapolis, IN: Hackett. (Original work published
in 1748)

Leavitt, S. D., & Dubner, S. J. (2005). *Freakonomics: A rogue economist
explores the hidden side of everything*. New York: William Morrow.

LeBar, L. E. (1987, January 1). What children owe to Comenius. *Christian
History & Biography, 13*(1), 19.

LeCompte, M. D., & Preissle, J. (1993). *Ethnography and qualitative design in
educational research* (2nd ed.). San Diego, CA: Academic.

Lee, J. (2006). Tracking achievement gaps and assessing the impact of
NCLB on the gaps: An in-depth look into national and state reading
and math outcome trends. Cambridge, MA: The Civil Rights Project at
Harvard University. Available: www.civilrightsproject.harvard.edu/
research/esea/nclb_naep_lee.pdf

Levinson, D. J. (1986). *Seasons of a man's life*. New York: Ballantine.

Levinson, D. J. (1997). *Seasons of a woman's life*. New York: Ballantine.

Lewin, T. (2006, February 8). Testing plan is gaining high ratings nationwide. *The New York Times*, p. A19.

Locke, J. (1994). *An essay concerning human understanding*. Buffalo, NY:
Prometheus. (Original work published 1690)

Loewen, J. W. (1996). *Lies my teacher told me: Everything your American History textbook got wrong*. New York: Touchstone.

Lounsbury, J. H., & Vars, G. F. (2003, November). The future of middle level
education: Optimistic and pessimistic views. *Middle School Journal,
35*(2), 6–14.

MacDonald, C. (2005, March 13). It's all work, little play in kindergarten.
Detroit News.

Maslow, A. (1987). *Motivation and personality* (3rd ed.). New York:
HarperCollins.

McLuhan, M., & Fiore, Q. (1967). *The medium is the massage*. New York:
Bantam.

Meier, D. (1999–2000, December/January). Educating a democracy: Standards and the future of public education. *Boston Review, 24*(1).

Meier, D. (2002). *The power of their ideas*. Boston: Beacon Press.

Merriam, S. (1998). *Qualitative research and case study applications in
education: A qualitative approach*. San Francisco: Jossey-Bass.

Meyer, R. J. (2002, July). Captives of the script: Killing us softly with phonics. *Language Arts, 79*(6), 452–461. Available: www.rethinkingschools. org/archive/17_04/capt174.shtml

Molnar, A. (Ed.). (2002). *School reform proposals: The research evidence.* Greenwich, CT: Information Age Publishing.

Montessori, M. (1984). *The absorbent mind.* New York: Dell.

Morse, R., Flanigan, S., & Yerkie, M. (2005, August 29). America's best colleges. *U.S. News & World Report, 139*(7), 78.

National Association for the Education of Young Children. (1987). *Standardized testing of young children 3 through 8 years of age.* Washington, DC: NAEYC.

National Association for the Education of Young Children & National Association for Early Childhood Specialists in State Departments of Education. (2003). *Early childhood curriculum, assessment, and program evaluation:* [Online joint position statement]. Available: www.naeyc. org/about/positions/pdf/pscape.pdf

National Association of Elementary School Principals. (2004, September/ October). Trends in education—Sept. 2004. *Principal, 84*(1), 50–52.

National Association of School Psychologists. (2005). NASP position statement on early childhood assessment [Online document]. Bethesda, MD: NASP. Available: www.nasponline.org/information/pospaper_eca.html

National Center for Education Statistics. (2003). *Violence in U.S. public schools: 2000 school survey on crime and safety—Statistical analysis report.* Washington, DC: Author.

National Commission on Excellence in Education. (1983). *A nation at risk.* Washington, DC: U.S. Government Printing Office.

Neill, A. S. (1995). *Summerhill School: A new view of childhood.* New York: St. Martin's Griffin.

Nichols, S. L., Glass, G. V., & Berliner, D. C. (2005, September). *High stakes testing and student achievement: Problems with the No Child Left Behind Act.* Tempe, AZ: Education Policy Studies Laboratory.

Noddings, N. (2005, September). What does it mean to educate the whole child? *Educational Leadership, 63*(1), 8–13.

Oakes, J. (2005). *Keeping track: How schools structure inequality.* New Haven, CT: Yale University Press.

Ohanian, S. (2003, December 1). Bush flunks school. *The Nation, 27*(19), 28–29.

Ohmann, R. (2000, January/February). Historical reflections on accountability. *Academe, 86*(1), 24–29. Available: www.aaup.org/publications/ Academe/2000/00jf/JF00ohma.htm

Olson, L. (2002, January 30). Law mandates scientific base for research. *Education Week, 21*(20), 1, 14–15.

Olson, L. (2005, July 13). Requests win more leeway under NCLB. *Education Week, 24*(42), 20–21.

Patel, J. (2005, May 8). Prescription stimulant abused by some students anxious for edge. *San Jose Mercury News.*

Perlstein, L. (2004, May 31). School pushes reading, writing reform. *The Washington Post,* p. A1.

Perrone, V. (1991). Position paper [Association for Childhood Education International]: On standardized testing. *Childhood Education, 67,* 132–142.

Pestalozzi, J. H. (1894). *How Gertrude teaches her children.* London: Swan Sonnenschein.

Piaget, J. (1975). *The child's conception of the world.* Totowa, NJ: Littlefield, Adams.

Piaget, J. (1998). *The child's conception of space.* London: Routledge.

Piaget, J. (2000). *The psychology of the child.* New York: Basic Books.

Plato. (1986). *The dialogues of Plato.* New York: Bantam.

Pope, D. C. (2003). *Doing school: How we are creating a generation of stressed out, materialistic, and miseducated students.* New Haven, CT: Yale University Press.

Pope, J. (2005, July 10). Time off before college can be worthwhile. Associated Press Wire Release.

Powell, A. G., Farrar, E., & Cohen, D. K. (1985). *The shopping mall high school.* Boston, MA: Houghton Mifflin.

Pulliam, J. D., & Van Patten, J. J. (1998). *History of education in America* (7th ed.). Englewood Cliffs, NJ: Prentice Hall.

Rapoport, J. L., Giedd, J. N., Blumenthal, J., Hamburger, S., Jeffries, N., Fernandez, T., et al. (1999). Progressive cortical change during adolescence in childhood-onset schizophrenia: A longitudinal MRI study. *Archives of General Psychiatry, 56*(7), 649–654.

Ravitch, D. (2003a). *The language police: How pressure groups restrict what students learn.* New York: Knopf.

Ravitch, D. (2003b, Spring). The test of time. *Education Next, 3*(2), 38.

Ravitch, D. (2003c, Fall). What Harry Potter can teach the textbook industry [Online article]. *Hoover Digest, 4.* Available: www.hooverdigest.org/034/ravitch.html

Reyher, K. (2005). NCLB: Accountable for what? *LBJ Journal Online.* Available: www.lbj/index.php?journal.org/option=content&task=view&id=384

Richmond, G. (1997). *The MicroSociety school: A real world in miniature.* New York: Harper and Row.

Rogers, C. R. (1994). *Freedom to learn.* Englewood Cliffs, NJ: Prentice Hall.

Rosenthal, R., & Jacobson, L. (2003). *Pygmalion in the classroom: Teacher expectation and pupils' intellectual development.* Norwalk, CT: Crown House Publishing.

Ross, J. B., & McLaughlin, M. M. (Eds.) (1977). *The portable Renaissance reader.* New York: Penguin.

Rothstein, R. (2004, November 2). Too young to test [Online article]. *American Prospect, 15*(11). Available: www.prospect.org/web/page. ww?section=root&name=ViewPrint&articleId=8774

Rousseau, J. J. (1953). *The confessions* (J. M. Cohen, Trans.). New York: Penguin. (Original work published in 1781)

Rousseau, J. J. (1979). *Emile, or on education* (A. Bloom, Trans.). New York: Basic Books. (Original work published 1762)

Rubalcava, M. (2004, Fall). Leaving children behind [Online article]. *Rethinking Schools Online, 9*(1). Available: www.rethinkingschools.org/special_reports/bushplan/leav191.shtml

Rubin, J. S. (1989, March). The Froebel-Wright kindergarten connection: A new perspective. *Journal of the Society of Architectural Historians, 48*(1), 24–37.

Ruddle, M. (2005, December 29). Character counts at Sparrows Point Middle School [Online article]. *The Dundalk Eagle.* Available: www.dundalkeagle.com/articles/2005/12/29/news/news01.txt

Segrue, M. (1995). *Great minds part I: Second edition: Ancient philosophy and faith: From Athens to Jerusalem, lecture eight: Republic Vi–X: The architecture of reality.* Springfield, VA: The Teaching Company.

Shah, I. (1993). *The pleasantries of the incredible Mullah Nasrudin.* New York: Penguin.

Shirer, W. L. (1990). *The rise and fall of the Third Reich.* New York: Simon & Schuster.

Siegel, D. (2001). *The developing mind: How relationships and the brain interact to shape who we are.* New York: Guilford Press.

Simpson, J. A., & Weiner, E. S. C. (Eds.). (1991). *The compact Oxford English Dictionary* (2nd ed.). Oxford, England: Oxford University Press.

Singer, D. G., & Singer, J. L. (1990). *The house of make-believe: Children's play and the developing imagination.* Cambridge, MA: Harvard University Press.

Sisk, C. L., & Foster, D. L. (2004, September 27). The neural basis of puberty and adolescence. *Nature Neuroscience, 7,* 1040–1047.

Sizer, T. (1997a). *Horace's hope: What works for the American high school.* Boston: Houghton Mifflin/Mariner.

Sizer, T. (1997b). *Horace's school: Redesigning the American high school.* Boston: Houghton Mifflin/Mariner.

Sizer, T. (2004). *Horace's compromise.* Boston, MA: Houghton Mifflin/Mariner.

Skinner, B. F. (2002). *Beyond freedom and dignity.* Indianapolis, IN: Hackett. (Original work published in 1971).

Sloan, D. (Ed.) (1985). *The computer in education: A critical perspective.* New York: Teachers College Press.

Steiner, R. (1995). *The kingdom of childhood: Introductory talks on Waldorf education*. Great Barrington, MA: Anthroposophic Press.

Steiner, R. (2000). *Practical advice to teachers*. Great Barrington, MA: Anthroposophic Press.

Steiny, J. (2005, October 9). Edwatch: Get over passive learning. *Providence Journal*. Available: www.middleweb.com/mw/news/activelearning.html

Stevenson, L. M., & Deasy, R. J. (2005). *Third space: When learning matters*. Washington, DC: Arts Education Partnership.

Sunderman, G. L. (2006). *The unraveling of No Child Left Behind: How negotiated changes transform the law*. Cambridge, MA: The Civil Rights Project at Harvard University.

Taylor, J. L., & Walford, R. (1972). *Simulation in the classroom*. New York: Penguin.

Tenenbaum, D. (2003, May 1). The U.S. response to Sputnik [Online article]. *The Why Files*. Available: http://whyfiles.org/047Sputnik/main2.html

Terryn, M. (2002). *Real old rap: Grade 8*. Core Knowledge Conference, Nashville, TN: Available: www.coreknowledge.org/CK/resrcs/lessons/02_8_RealOldRap.pdf

Texas Center for Educational Research. (2001, June). *Effective instruction in middle schools*. Austin: Texas Center for Educational Research.

Thompson, P. M., Giedd, J. N., Woods, R. P., MacDonald, D., Evans, A. C., Toga, A. W. (2000, March 9). Growth patterns in the developing brain detected by using continuum mechanical tensor maps. *Nature, 404*, 190–193.

Trotter, A. (2000, April 12). Schools build own ramp onto info highway. *Education Week, 19*(31), 14.

Ullman, E. (2005, November). Familiarity breeds content. *Edutopia Online*. Available: www.edutopia.org/magazine/ed1article.php?id=Art_1397&issue-nov_5

U.S. Census Bureau. (2002, July). *The big payoff: Educational attainment and synthetic estimates of work-life earnings*. Washington, DC: U.S. Department of Commerce.

U.S. Department of Education. (2002, January 7). *Executive summary: The No Child Left Behind Act of 2001*. Washington, DC: U.S. Department of Education.

U.S. Department of Education. (2003, December). *Identifying and implementing educational practices supported by rigorous evidence: A user friendly guide*. Washington, DC: Institute of Education Sciences.

Van Dusen, L. M., & Edmundson, R. S. (2003, October). *Findings of the comprehensive summative evaluation of the JA Job Shadow Program*. Logan, UT: Worldwide Institute for Research and Evaluation.

van Gennep, A. (1961). *The rites of passage*. Chicago: University of Chicago Press.

Vinovskis, M. A. (1998). *Overseeing the nation's report card: The creation and evolution of the national assessment governing board (NAGB)*. Washington, DC: U.S. Department of Education.

Vogler, K. E. (2003, March). An integrated curriculum using state standards in a high-stakes testing environment. *Middle School Journal, 34*(4), 5–10.

Von Zastrow, C., & Janc, H. (2004, March). *Academic atrophy: The condition of the liberal arts in America's public schools*. Washington, DC: Council for Basic Education.

Vygotsky, L. S. (1929). The problem of the cultural development of the child II. *The Pedagogical Seminary and Journal of Genetic Psychology, 36*(3), 415–432.

Wade, C. K. (2004, November 3). Short-order education. *Education Week, 24*(10), 3.

Wallis, C., Miranda, C. A., Rubiner, B. (2005, August 8). Is middle school bad for kids? *Time, 166*(6), 48–51.

Walters, J., & Gardner, H. (1986). The crystallizing experience: Discovery of an intellectual gift. In R. Sternberg & J. Davidson (Eds.), *Conceptions of giftedness*. New York: Cambridge University Press.

Wasley, P. A., Fine, M., Gladden, M., Holland, N. E., King, S. P., Mosak, E., & Powell, L. C. (2000). *Small schools: Great strides: A study of new small schools in Chicago*. New York: Bank Street College of Education.

Werner, H. (1980). *Comparative psychology of mental development*. New York: International Universities Press.

Whitehurst, G. J. (2001, September). Much too late. *Education Next, 1*(2), 9, 16–20.

Wigginton, E. (1973). *The Foxfire book: Hog dressing, log cabin building, mountain crafts and foods, planting by the signs, snake lore, hunting tales, faith healing, moonshining*. New York: Anchor.

Wikipedia. (n.d.). The social conception of discourse [Online section]. Discourse [Web page]. *Wikipedia, the Free Encyclopedia*. Retrieved February 18, 2006, from http://en.wikipedia.org/wiki/Discourse

Wilgoren, J. (2001, January 7). In a society of their own, children are learning. *The New York Times*, B9.

Williams, W. M., Blythe, T., White, N., Li, J., Sternberg, R. J., & Gardner, H. (1996). *Practical intelligence for school*. New York: HarperCollins College.

Wilson, N. (2005, December 14). Kids helping kids. *San Luis Obispo Tribune*. Available: www.sanluisobispo.com/mld/sanluisobispo/13402915.htm

Wiltz, S. M. (2005, July/August). Bridging the preK-elementary divide. *Harvard Education Letter*. Available: www.edletter.org/current/bridging.shtml

Winerip, M. (2005, October 5). One secret to better test scores: Make state reading tests easier. *The New York Times*, B11.

Winnicott, D. W. (1982). *Playing and reality*. London: Routledge.

Wisdom of the ages [Online article]. Available: http://members.aol.com/ tigerlink/quotes.htm

Yeche, C. P. (2005, September). *Mayhem in the middle*. Washington, DC: Thomas B. Fordham Institute.

Zehr, M. A. (2005, January 12). New York City offers Firefighting 101 at New York high school. *Education Week, 24*(18), 7.

Zepeda, S. J., & Mayers, R. S. (2002). A case study of leadership in the middle grades: The work of the instructional lead teacher. *RMLE Online, 25*(1), 1–11.

Zernike, K. (2000, October 23). No time for napping in today's kindergarten. *New York Times*, A1.

Index

Note: References to figures are followed by the letter *f*.

Abraham Lincoln Middle School, 124
Academic Achievement Discourse
  aspects of, 10–16
  defined, 9–10
  history of, 16–23, 17f
  keywords of, 32–33
  negative consequences, 23–32
  vs. Human Development Discourse, 38f
academic pressure, 142
accountability, 20–21, 58
achievement, 11
achievement gap, 89
ADD/ADHD, 79
Adderall, 27
adolescence, early, 111–112, 114–117
adolescence, middle and late, 138–139
adult interactions, 123–124

Advanced Placement courses, 137
advisory system, 124
African-American students, 29–30
Alexander, William, 111–112
America 2000, 22
apprenticeships, 146–147
arts education, 11, 23–24, 127–128
assessment methods, 40–41, 42–43
Association for Childhood Education International, 78
Auld, Janice, 100
Aviation High School, 144

behaviorism, 99
Benjamin Franklin Middle School, 129
Bergman, Ingmar, 95
The Best and the Brightest (Halberstam), 59

Binet, Alfred, 18
brain development
   about, 55–56
   early adolescence, 115–116
   early childhood, 72–73
   middle and late adolescence,
      138–139
Broad Meadows Middle School,
   131
bullying, 119, 122

*Cardinal Principles of Secondary
   Education* (NEA), 40
career academies, 145
career preparation, 154–155
Central Middle School, 129
charter schools, 144–145
children's museums, 106–107
Children with Specific Learning
   Disabilities Act, 58
*The Child's Conception of the
   World* (Piaget), 70–71
Clarkson School of Discovery,
   127–128
"closing the gap," 152–153
Coalition of Essential Schools,
   140, 143
Coles, Robert, 52
college-preperatory education,
   16 18, 136–137, 154
Comenius, John Amos, 48
Committee of Ten, 16–18
Committee on Secondary School
   Studies (1893), 16–18
community-based education,
   104–105
computers, 78–79
cooperative education, 148
core academic subject focus,
   23–24
Core Knowledge system, 100–101
Craig Montessori Elementary
   School, 106

critical thinking, 10
cultural differences, 30
culture, corporate-influenced, 16
curriculum
   core subject focus, 23–24
   fragmented, in middle school,
      119–120
   individualized, 41
   standardized, 12
   standards-based curriculum,
      88–89
   student participation in devel-
      oping, 124–125

decision making, 130
development, human, and
   schools, 37, 64–65, 156f–157f
Dewey, John, 51
Direct Instruction (DI), 24–25,
   99–100
discipline problems, 62–63
DISTAR (Direct Instruction System for Teaching Arithmetic
   and Reading), 99
drama, 11, 23–24, 127–128

early childhood education
   about, 69–70
   best practices, 81–86, 86f
   developmentally inappropriate
      practices, 75–80, 85, 86f
   developmental needs, 70–73
   main purpose of, 73–75
education, etymology of, 39
educational funding
   federal involvement, 20
   restricted access to, 25
educational release, 148–149
The Education of Man (Froebel),
   50–51
education professionals, 26–29,
   46–47
eidetic imagery, 72

1818 Report of the Commissioners for the University of Virginia, 39
Electrical Academy at Edison High School, 145
Elementary and Secondary Education Act, 20, 58
elementary school education
  about, 88–91
  best practices, 103–109
  developmentally inappropriate practices, 92f, 96–103
  developmental needs, 91–93, 92f
  main purpose of, 94–96
Eliot, Charles, 16
Elkind, David, 54, 76
Emile (Rousseau), 48–50
emotional connections, 120–121, 129–130, 131–132
Engelmann, Sigfried, 99
Enlightenment, 44
entrepreneurial enterprises, 146
equity, in education, 153
Erikson, Erik, 52, 96
estrogen, 115
Every Kid a Winner: Accountability in Education (Lessinger), 21
existentialism, 45
experiential, 40–41
Exploratorium, 107
Eyes to the Future, 125

fact-based learning, 100–101
FDNY High School for Fire and Life Safety, 144–145
federal government, 20–23
Flesch, Rudolf, 19
foreign language study, 11
Fox Cities Apprenticeship Program, 147
Foxfire Experiment, 104–105
Foxfire School, 105
Freud, Sigmund, 52
Froebel, Fredrich, 50–51

full-day kindergarten, 80

Gardner, Howard, 107
Gardner's theory of multiple intelligences, 97
Gates, Bill, 135–136
generativity, 59
Goals 2000: Educate America Act, 22
Goodall, Jane, 95
grade retention, 29–30
grading, 11–12, 30–31
growth and development, 31–32, 42–43

Hand Middle School, 128
happiness, 47
Harry Hurt Middle School, 125
Head Start, 20
health and wellness education, 128–129
Helen King Middle School, 125
Highland Elementary School, 97
high school education
  about, 135–137
  best practices, 142–149
  developmentally inappropriate practices, 140–142, 141f
  developmental needs, 138–139
Hirsch, E. D., Jr., 100–101
history instruction, 11, 102
homework, 79–80
How Gertrude Teaches Her Children (Pestalozzi), 50
Human Development Discourse
  about, 8, 34–36
  defined, 36–39
  history, 48–56, 49f
  keywords, 66–67
  positive consequences of, 56–66
  vs. Academic Achievement Discourse, 38f
humanism, 44–45

humanitarianism, 59
human potential, 60–61

imagination, 72
Improving America's Schools Act,
  23
independence, fostering, 141
individualized instruction, 12
Individuals with Disabilities Education Improvement Act (IDEA),
  20
information technology (IT), 10
interdisciplinary studies, 108
internships, 145–146
intimacy, 139
Iowa Test of Basic Skills, 18–19
ipsative assessment, 42–43

Jefferson, Thomas, 39
job shadowing, 148
John Morse Waldorf Methods
  School, 84

kindergartens, 50–51, 80
Knotty Oak Middle School, 127
Komensky, Jan Amos, 48
KURA-LP (98.9 FM), 146

labeling, 58
Laboratory School (Univ. of Chicago), 51
Lakeside High School, 146
Latino students, 29–30
learning, intrinsic value of, 30–31
learning styles, 12, 30
Lewis Middle School, 122
life skills education, 11
Lister, Joseph, 95
literature, 10, 102

Madison Junior High, 128
magnet schools, theme-based,
  144–145

Malaika Early Learning Center, 31
Marcus Aurelius, 47
Martin Luther King Jr. Middle
  School, 125
math instruction, 10, 75–77, 96–98
Math Understanding through the
  Science of Life, 125–126
Mayhem in the Middle (Fordham
  Institute), 112–113
mentoring, 147
Metropolitan Achievement Test,
  18
MicroSociety schools, 103–104
middle school education
  about, 111–113
  best practices, 121–132
  developmentally inappropriate
    practices, 114f, 117–121
  developmental needs, 114–117
Montessori, Maria, 52–53
Montessori Schools, 105–106
multiple intelligences, Gardner's
  theory of, 97
multiple intelligences curricula,
  108
"mumble strategy," 90
music education, 11, 23–24,
  127–128
myelination, 72
Myers Elementary School, 104
"My Pedagogic Creed" (Dewey),
  51

National Assessment of Educa-
  tional Progress, 20, 58
National Association for the
  Education of Young Children
  (NAEYC), 77
National Commission on Excel-
  lence in Education, 21
National Defense Education Act,
  20
A Nation at Risk, 21–22, 35

No Child Left Behind Act of 2001, 8–9, 20, 36

Oakland Health and Bioscience Academy, 145
Oakland Technical High School, 145
Opal School, 107

Papert, Seymour, 78
parent involvement, 126
pedagogy
    in high school, 140–142
    innovation and diversity in, 63–64
    and research, 14, 24, 43–46
Pestalozzi, Johann Heinrich, 50
phenomenology, 45
phonics, 19, 98
physical education, 11
physiognomic perception, 71
Piaget, Jean, 54, 70–71, 76, 91–92
plagiarism, 26
play, importance in childhood, 73–75
politicians
    control and power, 15, 27–28, 46
portfolios, 77
Portland Children's Museum, 107
positivism, 44
Practical Intelligence for School project, 127
problem solving, 10
project-based learning, 108
puberty, onset, 114–117

Rabun Gap-Nacoochee School, 104–105
readiness, 13
reading instruction, 10, 19, 75–77, 96–98
"real world" preparation, 139, 142, 154–155

recess, 80
Reggio Emilia schools, 82–83
relationships, student-adult, 123–124
Republic (Plato), 48
research data, and pedagogy, 14, 24, 43–46, 68
retention, grade, 29–30
Richmond, George, 103–104
Ritalin, 27
rites of passage, 116–117
role models, positive, 125–126
Romantic period, 44–45
Roseville Community Preschool (RCP), 81–82
Rousseau, Jean-Jacques, 48–50

safety, school, 119, 122–123
Salem High School, 146
school size, 118–119, 123
science education, 10
scripted teaching programs, 99–100
self-fulfilling prophecies, 61
service learning, 147
sex education, 128–129
"shopping mall high school," 140
simulated classrooms, 108
Sizer, Theodore, 140
social development, 56–58
social sciences, 11
Sparrows Point Middle School, 122
special education, 58
Sputnik I launch, 19–20
standardized testing
    about, 11–12
    artificiality of, 40
    in early childhood, 77–78
    history of, 18
    teaching to the test, 25
standards-based curriculum, 88–89

Standford-Binet intelligence test, 18
Stanford Achievement Test, 18
Steiner, Rudolf, 53–54
stress, 28–29
students
  cheating and plagiarizing, 26
  emotional connection and growth, 120–121, 129–130, 131–132
  empowerment, 130
  illegal performance aids used by, 27
  metacognition, 126–127
  social problems, 59–60, 62–63
  stress, 28–29
  student-adult relationships, 123–124
  student-teacher roles, 143–144
  varied strengths of, 57–58
synesthesia, 71–72

Talent Middle School, 130
teachers
  empowerment of, 61–62
  student-teacher roles, 143–144
  substitutes, 119
teaching to the test, 25
Teller, Edward, 19
Terman, Lewis, 18–19

testosterone, 115
textbooks, 101–103
thematic instruction, 108
Thorndike, Edward L., 18–19
Tolenas Elementary School, 105
tracking, 140–141
Turning Points 2000: Educating Adolescents in the 21st Century, 120

van Dyke, Henry, 47
violence, in schools, 119, 122–123
vocational education, 11
Vygotsky, Lev, 54–55

Walden III Middle School, 132
Waldorf Education, 53–54, 83–85
Weaving Resources program, 106–107
Webb Middle School, 130, 132
Werner, Heinz, 71
West Hawaii Explorations Academy, 144
Why Johnny Can't Read (Flesch), 19
Wigginton, Eliot, 104–105
worksheets, 101–103
writing instruction, 10, 96–98, 130–131

About the Author

Thomas Armstrong is a former teacher and the author of 13 books, including *In Their Own Way, 7 Kinds of Smart, The Myth of the A.D.D. Child,* and the ASCD books *Multiple Intelligences in the Classroom* (2nd ed.), *Awakening Genius in the Classroom, The Multiple Intelligences of Reading and Writing,* and *ADD/ADHD Alternatives in the Classroom.* His books have been translated into 21 languages. He can be contacted at P.O. Box 548, Cloverdale, CA 95425. E-mail: thomas@thomasarmstrong.com. Web site: www.thomasarmstrong.com. Fax: 707-894-4474.